Ancient Greece and Rome

Reader

Core Knowledge®

ISBN: 978-1-68380-322-5

Ancient Greece and Rome

Table of Contents

Ancient Greece and Rome
Reader
Core Knowledge History and Geography™

Chapter 1
The Ancient Greek City-States

A Great Civilization Many people believe that the greatest of all the civilizations of the ancient world was the civilization of Greece. However, it is a little misleading to speak about ancient Greece as though it were a single civilization.

The Big Question

What different forms of government were adopted by various city-states?

Ancient Greece was not a unified country. It was a collection of independent **city-states**. The ancient Greek word for city-state was *polis* (/poh* lihs/). A typical polis would have included a town or a small city and the farmlands surrounding it. Most Greek city-states had a population of no more than twenty thousand and covered an area of only a hundred or so square miles.

Vocabulary

city-state, n. a city that is an independent political state with its own ruling government

Asia Minor, n. a peninsula in southwestern Asia; today most of this area is the country of Turkey

By 500 BCE, dozens of these city-states existed, mainly along the shores of the Aegean Sea. Most were located in the area of present-day Greece, but others were scattered along the coast of **Asia Minor**, on the shores of the Black Sea, in southern Italy, and in northern Africa.

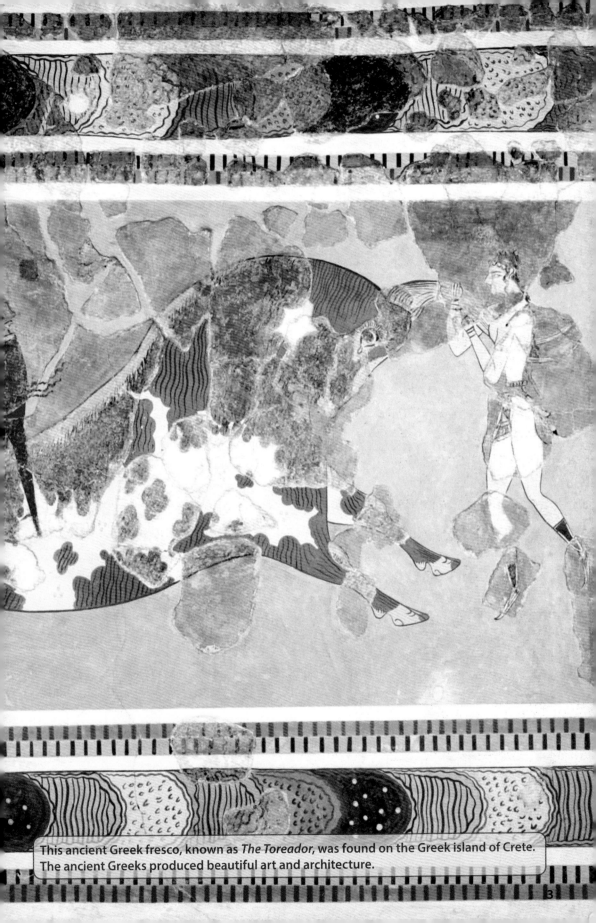

This ancient Greek fresco, known as *The Toreador*, was found on the Greek island of Crete. The ancient Greeks produced beautiful art and architecture.

The Greek city-states had a number of things in common. First, the people of the city-states all spoke Greek, though dialects varied from city-state to city-state. (A dialect is a regional variety of a language.) The Greeks referred to non-Greek speakers as "barbarians." The word comes from another Greek word —*bárbaros*—meaning to babble. When these people spoke, the Greeks could hear only meaningless syllables that sounded to them like *bar, bar, bar*.

The Greek city-states were also unified by religion. The citizens of the various city-states worshiped the same set of Greek gods. Zeus (/zooss/) was the chief god, but he shared power with other gods, including his wife Hera (/hihr*uh/), the sun god Apollo (/uh*pahl*oh/), the sea god Poseidon (/poh*sye*dun/), and the love goddess Aphrodite (/af*ruh*dye*tee/). The Greeks believed that these gods lived on Mount Olympus but came down from time to time to influence

This ancient sculpted wall decoration, called a frieze, can be found on the Parthenon in Athens, Greece. The frieze depicts some of the Assembly of the Gods. From left to right you can see Poseidon, Apollo, and Artemis, the goddess of the hunt.

4

human affairs. They told marvelous stories, or myths, about the adventures and misadventures of their gods. They built temples to honor their gods.

Greek city-states also came together for athletic competitions like the Olympic Games, which you will read about in Chapter 4. But each Greek city-state was also unique. Each had its own traditions, legends, and local heroes. Almost all city-states worshiped a handful of local gods along with the central gods.

Different Governments

Each city-state also had its own distinctive form of government. In fact, the Greeks were so innovative, or groundbreaking, when it came to government and politics that many of the words we use to talk about these subjects today can be traced back to ancient Greek words. Our words *politics* and *police officer* are both derived from the word *polis*. Politics is the art of governing a polis, or state, and a police officer is a person who helps preserve order in the state.

In the beginning, most Greek city-states were ruled by kings. However, by 500 BCE, most city-states had adopted other forms of government, including **tyranny**, **aristocracy**, **oligarchy** (/ahl*ih*gahr*kee/), and **democracy**.

Tyranny was a system in which one man was the dictator—someone who held all the power. For Greeks, tyranny was different from **monarchy**: tyrants seized power illegally, whereas kings inherited the throne legally. Some tyrants were

> ## Vocabulary
>
> **tyranny,** n. a type of government in which one person illegally seizes all power, usually ruling in a harsh and brutal way; a dictatorship
>
> **aristocracy,** n. the upper or noble class whose members' status is usually inherited
>
> **oligarchy,** n. a government controlled by a small group of people made up of aristocratic and wealthy non-aristocratic families
>
> **democracy,** n. in ancient Greece, a form of government in which the male citizens held ruling power and made decisions; in modern times, a form of government in which citizens choose the leaders by vote
>
> **monarchy,** n. a government led by a king or a queen

Map of Ancient Greece, 500 BCE

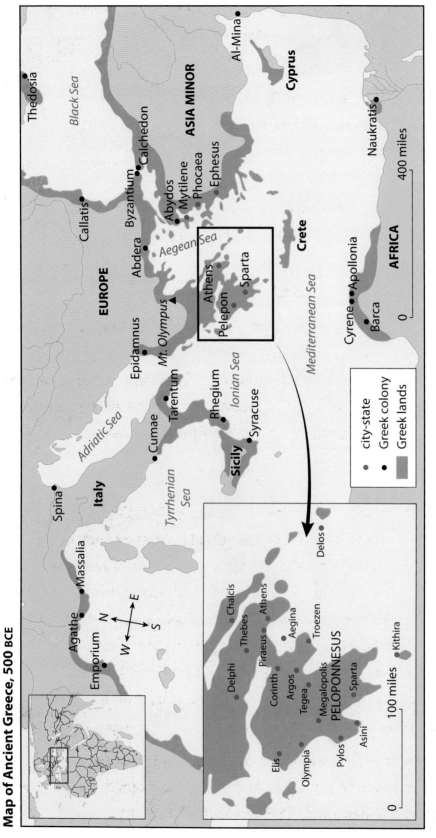

The Greeks established colonies throughout the Mediterranean. This map shows the extent of ancient Greece around 500 BCE.

popular because they opposed the rich and helped the poor. However, few Greeks wanted to live under tyrants all the time.

Aristocracy was a system in which a few noble, or upper-class, families held power. The word *aristocracy* actually means rule of the best. Sometimes these "best" families shared power with an **assembly** made up of citizens, but not always.

Vocabulary

assembly, n. a group of people; in ancient Greece, the Assembly made laws

An oligarchy was similar to aristocracy. Again, the power was held by only a few people. In fact, *oligarchy* means rule of the few. But in this case, the few were not only noble families but also wealthy men. (Often oligarchies were comprised of aristocratic and wealthy nonaristocratic families.)

Finally, there was democracy. In a democracy, power was shared by a large number of male citizens. Citizens took part in debates, decided government policy, and elected officials. The Greeks seem to have been the first people to experiment with this kind of government. The experiment eventually caught on, and democracy became the pattern of government in a number of Greek city-states.

Lack of Unity

The Greeks were proud of the independence and individuality of their city-states. They thought it was better to live under local government than under the power of a king who lived far away. However, there were also disadvantages to the city-state model. The Greek city-states were frequently getting into disagreements and wars. This lack of unity made it easier for foreign countries to invade Greece. In times of crisis, the city-states might join together to fight a common enemy, but this was the exception, not the rule. In general, the alliances among city-states tended to be short-lived, while the rivalries among them tended to be long-lasting.

One of the greatest rivalries was between Athens and Sparta, two of the largest and most powerful city-states. In the next two chapters, you will read about these two city-states and the differences between them.

Chapter 2
Athens

Athenian Democracy Athens was one of the largest of the Greek city-states and also one of the most democratic. Today, we remember it as the birthplace of democracy.

The Big Question

In what ways was Athenian democracy limited?

Athenian democracy developed gradually. Over many decades, monarchy gave way to aristocracy, aristocracy to oligarchy, and then oligarchy to democracy. The Athenians also had to get rid of a few tyrants. Over the years, more and more people won the right to participate in government. By 500 BCE, a recognizably democratic system was firmly established.

At the center of Athenian democracy was the Assembly. The Assembly passed laws, imposed taxes, and voted on issues of war and peace. All Athenian male citizens were allowed to participate in the Assembly. Before deciding an issue, the members of the Assembly would debate the proposal. Then they would vote by holding up their hands. If a majority of those present supported the proposal, it would be accepted.

Vocabulary

citizen, n. a person who is legally recognized as a member or subject of a country or state

In Athens, the Assembly debated and voted on issues.

This *ostrakon* had the name "Themistocles" scratched on it.

The Assembly also had the power to **ostracize**, or banish, citizens who might pose a danger to the polis. Again, this was done by voting. During ostracism votes, each citizen was allowed to scratch another citizen's name on a piece of pottery called an *ostrakon*. If enough people scratched the same name, the ostracized citizen had to leave the city-state and stay away for ten

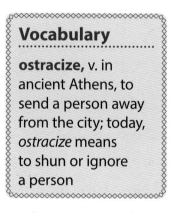

years. However, he was allowed to keep his property, and at the end of ten years, he was allowed to return.

The Assembly was assisted by a smaller council, called the Boule (/boo*lee/), which was made up of five hundred members chosen by lot. Each member served a year-long term, and no citizen could serve more than two terms. The Boule decided which issues needed to be brought before the Assembly and which ones could be handled by other officials.

The Legal System

The legal system was also quite democratic. Athenian law was divided into two sections. There were public laws, which had to do with the city-state, and private laws through which people could work out their disagreements. If someone broke a public law, he would have to pay a fine or face the penalty that had been decided upon by the Assembly or by the Boule. If someone had a disagreement with a neighbor, he could take his neighbor to a law court near the marketplace and have a **jury** decide his case.

Athenian juries were larger than ours are today. In some cases, as many as 501 citizens sat on a single jury! The idea behind these giant juries was to reduce the risk of bribery and **corruption**: it is easier to bribe a dozen jurors than it is to pay off several hundred. Because the juries were so big, nearly all citizens served on juries at some point in their lives. Jury members voted by placing tokens, called hubs, in a jar. Solid hubs stood for "not guilty," and hollow hubs meant "guilty."

The fourth element of Athenian democracy was a board of ten generals known as the *strategoi* (/strat*uh*goi/). These generals directed the army. They were elected each year by a tribe, or group, to the Assembly. There were ten groups in all.

Limits of Athenian Democracy

It is important to understand that Athens was not completely democratic by modern standards. You read earlier that all Athenian citizens were allowed to participate in the Assembly. However, not everyone in the polis was a citizen. To qualify as a citizen, a person had to be:

- male
- at least eighteen years of age
- not enslaved
- the son of two Athenian parents

> ## Vocabulary
>
> **jury,** n. a group of people who listen to information presented during a trial in a court and make decisions about whether someone is guilty or innocent
>
> **corruption,** n. illegal or dishonest behavior, often by people in a position of power

Women, children, enslaved people, and foreigners living in Athens were not citizens. Therefore, they could not vote in the Assembly or serve on juries.

Although Athenian women played an important role in religious affairs, they had almost no political rights. They could not own property. They were always under the control of a male relative, such as a husband, father, brother, or even an adult son. This male relative decided whom the

This ancient Greek stone carving shows a woman working in her home.

woman would marry. If her husband died, she could be remarried without her consent. Sometimes, if a husband knew he was dying, he would decide before his death whom his wife should marry next! Women could not participate in debates in the Assembly. They could not attend certain public events. Girls might receive some education at home, but they were not sent to school. Instead of participating in polis politics, women were expected to bear children and tend to their families. The family was very important in ancient Athens, and Athenian women were expected to uphold it.

As a busy trading city, Athens opened its doors to many foreigners. These foreign residents, known as *metics* (/met*ihks/), played an important role in the Athenian economy. Many metics were artisans, craftsmen, or merchants. Although some metics were presented with honorary citizenship, most never became citizens.

Enslaved people had it even worse. They made up as much as a quarter or a third of the population. A rich citizen might have hundreds of enslaved workers to run his household, farm, or business. A smaller household might have between ten and fifty. Only the poor did not depend on slave labor. Enslaved workers cleaned, shopped, cooked, carried water, washed clothing, and helped raise children. Some enslaved workers were educated, so they could help teach the children in a family. Others were accomplished musicians who provided entertainment. But even the most talented enslaved person lacked any political rights. Although Athenian enslaved workers could sometimes buy their freedom, they could not purchase Athenian citizenship.

Because of these requirements, only about forty thousand of the nearly three hundred thousand people living in Athens and the surrounding countryside qualified as citizens. So Athenian democracy definitely had its limits. Still, we should not dismiss what the Athenians achieved. In 500 BCE, you could not find another place where so many of the people were involved in political affairs. Later societies would carry democratic ideals even further, but it was the Athenians who took the all-important first steps.

Athenian Education

Because the Athenians believed that every citizen should play a role in the government of the city-state, they took pains to prepare young men to become good citizens. They believed a good education would benefit the polis as well as the individual.

A citizen needed to be able to take part in debates in the Assembly and law courts. He also needed to know how to argue, how to defend his own opinions, and how to criticize the ideas of others. This is why the Athenians taught their sons **rhetoric**.

Along with rhetoric, Athenian schools taught **logic**, reading, writing, arithmetic, and music. Boys learned to play a stringed instrument called the lyre and memorized sections from two **epic poems** attributed to the ancient Greek poet Homer, The *Iliad* and The *Odyssey*.

> ### Vocabulary
>
> **rhetoric,** n. the skill of using words effectively in speaking or writing
>
> **logic,** n. the study of ways of thinking and making well-reasoned arguments
>
> **"epic poem,"** (phrase) a long poem that tells the story of a hero's adventures

This painted vase depicts a classroom in ancient Greece.

In addition to academic instruction, every young man was given two years of military instruction and many years of physical education. Athenian men were expected to exercise in a gymnasium. This was not an enclosed building, like a modern gym, but a parklike area outside the city where men gathered in the cool shade of the trees to exercise their bodies and relax their minds. The men did not wear clothes when they exercised. In fact, the word *gymnasium* comes from a Greek word meaning "to exercise naked." In addition to exercising, they competed in athletic competitions.

When an Athenian male got a little older, he might go to a symposium. A symposium was like a banquet. Citizens gathered to eat, drink, listen to musicians, converse, and enjoy one another's company. Much wine was consumed, but many symposiums also had an educational purpose. When the members of a symposium settled down for conversation, the men took turns speaking on a chosen theme, such as love or happiness. The participants were not just gossiping or wasting time. They were sharing wisdom and reaching conclusions.

Athenian education sought to produce loyal Athenian citizens, but it also sought to produce cultured, well-rounded men who appreciated art, music, and sports. The ideal citizen would be equally comfortable on the battlefield or in the Assembly. He would be willing to follow army discipline during wartime but also willing to drink wine and eat a hearty dinner at a symposium when the war was over. He would fulfill his political responsibilities but also pursue other interests. In short, the Athenian educational system was designed to produce solid citizens and well-rounded individuals.

Chapter 3
Sparta

Military Culture In the city-state of Sparta, less than one hundred miles southwest of Athens, there was a very different idea about the purpose of education. Spartans raised their children to be warriors. They had no interest in developing "well-rounded individuals," or individuals of any sort.

The Big Question

Why were Spartan children, especially boys, treated so harshly?

The Spartan educational system emphasized military training, almost from the cradle to the grave. For example, the Athenians required two years of military training, but the Spartans required twenty-three!

When a Spartan woman gave birth to a baby boy, the child was inspected by a government committee. If the baby was healthy and looked as if he might grow into a strong warrior, he was allowed to live. However, if the baby seemed weak or unhealthy, he was often left outdoors to die.

The Spartans made sure children grew up to be tough. Spartan children who cried were not picked up or comforted. The Spartans believed that soothing children in this way made them soft. A similar objection was raised against sandals—wearing shoes meant that boys would have soft feet. Soldiers needed tough feet. Therefore, Spartan boys had to go barefoot, even in the dead of winter.

Spartan warriors, like the one shown here, were the best-trained soldiers of their time.
The inset image is a bronze statue of a Spartan soldier from the 500s BCE.

At the age of seven, Spartan boys were sent away from their families to begin military training. They lived in **barracks** with other boys their age and were taught to obey without question. Even the slightest questioning of authority brought a severe whipping.

In Sparta, little time was spent teaching reading, writing, and poetry. Instead, physical fitness was king. Spartan boys were taught to endure great pain and never accept defeat. When the boys became teenagers, their food rations were cut so that they would have to learn to find food for themselves—this included stealing.

Young men could marry at age twenty, but they had to continue sleeping in the barracks until they turned thirty. They had to sneak away to be with their wives, and they were punished if they got caught. Even after they moved in with their wives, they had to eat with their army unit rather than with their wives and children. Military service continued until the men turned sixty.

The entire Spartan state was organized as a military unit, and everyone had a role to play. Spartan women did not fight, but they had more political rights than Athenian women. They could own land, and they were encouraged to take part in footraces and other sports so that they would be healthy mothers. Once they became mothers, they were expected to help raise their sons to be warriors.

Spartan mothers had to be prepared to lose their sons in war.

This bronze statue of a Spartan woman running is from the 500s BCE. Spartan women were encouraged to run to keep fit.

On hearing that her son had died in battle, one Spartan woman refused to weep. Instead, she announced her loss proudly: "I bore him so that he might die for Sparta, and that is what has happened, as I wished."

Why did the Spartans place so much emphasis on military skill and bravery? It was partly to protect themselves against foreign enemies. When someone suggested that Sparta build a wall around the city, the legendary Spartan leader Lycurgus (/lie*ker*gis/) supposedly replied that a "wall of men" would protect the city more effectively than any wall of bricks.

But there was another reason too. The Spartans ruled over large numbers of enslaved people called *helots*. The first helots were captured in war. Like serfs in feudal Europe centuries later, helots were tied to the land, forced to work on state-owned farms. They were assigned to individual Spartans, but could not be bought and sold by these masters. Whatever they grew or produced on the land, they owed their masters a portion of it.

The life of a helot in Sparta, in most cases, was much worse than the life of an enslaved person in Athens. In fact, Spartans made fun of the Athenians for coddling their enslaved workers. The Spartans said that in Athens, you could hardly tell the enslaved workers from the citizens. That was not a problem in Sparta. Although the helots outnumbered Spartan citizens by perhaps twenty to one, the Spartans had a reputation for treating them harshly. There are many historical accounts that say the helots were beaten regularly and could be put to death for complaining. However, there are some accounts that describe the Spartans as being a little more reasonable at times. They may even have allowed some helots the right to own property and fight alongside Spartans in battle.

Despite the harsh rules, (or perhaps because of them), the helots sometimes rose in revolt. That was another reason the Spartans forced all male citizens to be warriors.

Spartan education was cruel and inhuman by today's standards. But Spartans valued the results that came from these methods. Spartan citizens were patriotic, disciplined, and tough. They valued equality between Spartan citizens. They were taught to care more about the well-being of the state than about their own personal well-being. And they were matchless fighters, willing to defend their polis to the death.

Spartan Government

The government of Sparta is generally called an oligarchy, but it also contained elements of monarchy, aristocracy, and very limited democracy. The Spartans had not one but two kings. These two men were supposed to prevent each other from becoming corrupt tyrants. They were also in charge of the all-important army. In addition to the kings, Sparta also had

The disciplined and well-trained Spartan soldiers were more than a match for other armies.

an **aristocratic council** of elders and an Assembly. Sparta's Assembly, though, was far less democratic than the one in Athens. Citizens were not allowed to debate an issue, only to approve or disapprove a proposal, and they showed their approval or disapproval not with a show of hands but by shouting for or against a measure.

Vocabulary

"aristocratic council," (phrase) a group of people from the upper class or nobility who helped govern Sparta

Spartan elections were handled in the same way. Citizens were called together in an open field and asked to shout for the candidate they preferred. Judges determined which candidate got the loudest shouts. (The Athenians found all this shouting very humorous.)

Although the Spartans accepted a few democratic ideas, they were generally doubtful about Athenian-style democracy. They believed that their way of life was better than the Athenian way of life.

Contrasting Lifestyles

Athenians enjoyed going to symposiums, or banquets, with good food and wine. The Spartans were less extravagant and believed in keeping life simple. Athenian writers wrote that Spartan cooks were told not to make the food too tasty. Apparently, they succeeded. After eating dinner in Sparta, one visitor said, "Now I know why they aren't afraid to die in battle!" The only "fun" activity the Spartans allowed was dancing, and this was only tolerated because the elders thought dancing improved a soldier's footwork. However, it is important to note that a lot of what we know about Sparta comes from the Athenians, and they were more than a little biased!

The Athenians trained their citizens to be skilled in rhetoric and public speaking. Spartans, on the other hand, were famous for avoiding long speeches. You may know the English word *laconic*. This word means concise, or of few words. What you may not know is that in ancient Greece, *laconic* was a synonym for *Spartan*—and the word itself comes from *Laconia*, the name of the territory where Sparta was located. The Spartans were famous for their brief replies. Once a Greek from a hostile city-state told a Spartan, "If we defeat you, we will destroy your city." The Spartan spoke only one word in reply: "If." Now that's laconic!

Athens was a culturally rich city that eventually produced some of the greatest art and literature of all time. A great Athenian statesman once explained that Athenians saw no conflict between strength and beauty: "Our love of what is beautiful does not lead to extravagance; our love of the things of the mind does not make us soft." By contrast, the Spartans worried that too much attention to the "things of the mind" might make them soft. They chose to produce soldiers, not artists.

Athens was located only four miles from the sea, but Sparta was an inland city. This inland location may have encouraged the Spartans to isolate themselves from the rest of the world. Whatever the reason, that is what they tried to do. While Athens welcomed foreigners, Sparta tried to keep them away so that they could preserve their traditional ways and highly ordered society. The Spartans even avoided using silver and gold coins, because these had a tendency to attract foreign merchants. Instead, they used iron bars, which nobody but a Spartan could possibly want.

Location also helped determine the military differences between these two city-states. The **landlocked** Spartans generally had a small navy, or none at all, but their army was the best in Greece. The Spartan army often fought using a military formation known as the **phalanx**. The phalanx formation was made up of many soldiers in a tight, dense group, armed with spears and shields. They moved together as one. The success of this formation in battle depended greatly on constant

Vocabulary

landlocked, adj. cut off from the seacoast; surrounded by land

phalanx, n. a group of soldiers who attack in close formation with their shields overlapping and spears pointed forward

drilling, discipline, courage, patriotism, and the idea of equality. The phalanx in many ways defined Spartan society.

Athens tried to excel in both land and sea warfare, but the Athenian navy was especially strong.

Sparta and Athens were so different that each city-state was suspicious of the other, and it was hard for the two to get along. The rivalry between these two city-states would play an important role in Greek history. In the next few chapters, you will read about a couple of occasions when Athens and Sparta managed to cooperate and also about a fateful war in which they confronted one another on the battlefield.

Athens had a large, powerful fleet of ships.

Chapter 4
The Olympic Games

Sports Obsession Athens and Sparta were not the only Greek city-states that had trouble getting along. Many city-states fought and feuded with each other. However, the Greeks did manage to lay their quarrels aside for a few things, and one of those things was sports.

The Big Question

What were the Olympic Games?

One of the most famous athletic competitions was held in the city of Olympia, not far from Sparta. The Olympic Games were held every fourth year. Several months before the games began, a sacred engraved disk—the **emblem** of the games—was carried to all the Greek city-states that were expected to compete. The messenger who brought the disk would inform everyone when the games would be held. The messenger would also explain the terms of the Olympic **truce**. The city-states agreed to stop fighting during the time it took for athletes to travel to Olympia, attend the games, and return home again—a period of one to three months.

Vocabulary

emblem, n. a symbol

truce, n. an agreement to stop fighting

This image is an artist's impression of athletes competing in a footrace in the ancient Greek Olympic Games. The inset image (above) shows a footrace depicted on a Greek pot from the 400s BCE. Generally, athletes competed without clothing.

In the Beginning

The Olympic Games began as part of a religious festival in honor of Zeus, the king of the Greek gods. The festival originally included processions and religious ceremonies. In 776 BCE, a footrace was added. Contestants ran the length of the stadium, about two hundred yards. Later, additional events were added, and the Olympic Games became a regular occurrence.

The official prize for winning an athletic event at the Olympics was a wreath of olive leaves, which was placed on the head of the victor. But the real prize was honor. A victorious athlete would almost certainly become a hero in his native city-state. He might even be **immortalized** in songs or sculptures.

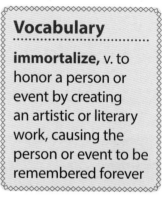

Vocabulary

immortalize, v. to honor a person or event by creating an artistic or literary work, causing the person or event to be remembered forever

When an athlete won an event, he received a wreath of olive leaves.

Competitors in the early Olympics generally dressed as the Athenians did in their gymnasiums, which is to say they wore no clothing at all—not even shoes! The Greeks did not mind a little nudity, and the runners didn't want to be slowed down by clothing.

The spectators sat on sloping hillsides near the stadium, watching and cheering for their favorite athletes. But only free Greek males and unmarried **priestesses** were allowed to watch. Other women and enslaved people who were caught watching could be put to death.

Greek citizens came to the games from all parts of the known world. Like modern sports fans, they came to marvel at athletic excellence and experience the thrill of victory. They cheered for the athletes of their own city-state and for skillful athletes from other city-states.

Early Athletic Events

Most of the original athletic contests were based on physical skills that the ancient Greeks needed for survival. Because there were many wars, it was important that Greek men learn to throw the javelin (a kind of spear), run quickly, wrestle well, and ride a horse.

At least two of the early Olympic events involved throwing the javelin. In one competition, athletes threw the javelin for distance; in another they threw for accuracy. In this last event, it appears that competitors had to throw the javelin at a target while galloping past it on a horse. This required strength, balance, and coordination.

Another event was the discus throw. The discus was shaped like a Frisbee and was made of stone, iron, lead, or bronze. Each discus weighed about fourteen pounds. Athletes competed to see who could throw the discus the farthest. To throw a discus, the athlete had to hold it tucked in his hand, swing it back and then forward, and release it at just the right time.

The long jump was meant to see who could jump the farthest. Unlike today's long jump, the ancient Greek athletic event involved carrying weights while jumping. The weights were made of stone or metal. They were shaped like dumbbells and weighed four to eight pounds each.

The pentathlon was an athletic competition that consisted of five different events: discus, javelin, long jump, wrestling, and a two hundred-yard footrace.

The pankration (/pahn*krah*tee*awn/) was a kind of wrestling event that had only two rules. Biting your opponent and sticking your fingers into your opponent's eyes were not allowed. Competitors were allowed to twist arms, throw punches, and generally beat up on their opponents.

Many different kinds of footraces were held. In addition to the two hundred-yard race, there was a four hundred-yard race, and another competition in which competitors had to run four hundred yards while wearing helmets and shin guards and carrying a shield.

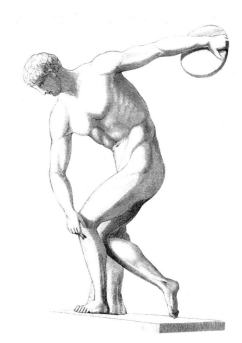

The Discobolus, or *The Discus Thrower*, is a famous Greek sculpture by a sculptor known as Myron (480–440 BCE).

Pankration was a combination of boxing and wrestling, but with very few rules.

Down Through the Ages

The Olympic Games continued for centuries, even through much of the time that the Roman Empire ruled Greece. Finally, in 393 CE, after more than a thousand years of competition, the Roman emperor Theodosius I (/thee*oh*doh*shee*us/) canceled the games. He was a Christian and did not like the religious **rites** in honor of Zeus that were still a part of the Olympics.

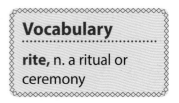
It was not until the late 1800s that the games resumed. The first of the modern Olympic Games were held in 1896, in a new stadium built in Athens. Ever since, the Olympics have been held every four years, except during World War I and World War II. People from all over the world participate. The modern games include many more events than the ancient games, and they do not include any religious rites. But the ancient Greek love of physical fitness, skill, and courage lives on in today's Olympics.

Just as they did thousands of years ago, every four years athletes compete against each other in the Olympic Games.

Chapter 5
The Persian Wars

The Beginning of the War In the first chapter, you learned that there were a number of Greek city-states on the coast of Asia Minor. About 546 BCE, these city-states came under the control of the Persians, who appointed harsh tyrants to rule each city-state.

The Big Question
....

Why do you think the Spartans and the Athenians joined together to fight the Persians in the later battles of the Persian Wars?

Around 499 BCE, the city-state of Miletus (/mye*leet*us/) rebelled against Persian rule. The people of Miletus asked the Greeks in other city-states to help them overthrow the Persians. The Spartans refused, but the Athenians agreed to help.

In 498 BCE, the Athenians crossed the Aegean Sea to Asia Minor. They conquered the Persian-controlled city of Sardis. When the other Greek city-states in Asia Minor learned of Athens's victory, they decided to join the revolt against the Persians. The Athenians felt their point had been made, and they went home. Within three years, the Persian king Darius had put down the revolt and regained control of the Greek city-states in Asia Minor.

Even though they had regained control of their empire, the Persians were angry with the Athenians. In 490 BCE, the Persians crossed the Aegean Sea to punish the Athenians.

Ancient stone carving of a trireme

The Greek trireme was a galley ship that had three layers of oars. These ships were used against the Persians.

Marathon

The Athenians and met the Persians on the plain at Marathon, about twenty-six miles from Athens. The Athenians were badly outnumbered, but they decided to attack. The Greek charge was a success. The Persians broke ranks and fled to their ships, and the Greeks cut them down as they ran. By the end of the battle, more than six thousand Persians were dead, while only 192 Greeks had fallen.

According to legend, the Greeks ordered a messenger to run to Athens and deliver news of the victory. The messenger ran the twenty-six miles to Athens, gasped out his victory announcement, "Rejoice, we conquer!", and died of exhaustion. Today, we use the word *marathon* to refer to a 26.2-mile footrace.

Marathon was an extremely important battle. Because the Athenians won, they were filled with self-confidence. They began to think that they were the most powerful of all the Greeks.

The story of the messenger inspired the modern-day marathon race.

Thermopylae

The Persians were not yet done with the Athenians, however. In 480 BCE, another Persian army was sent to defeat the Greeks. With an army of more than one hundred thousand men, as well as six hundred to seven hundred ships, the Persian king Xerxes (/zurk*seez/) (486–465 BCE) was determined to conquer all of Greece.

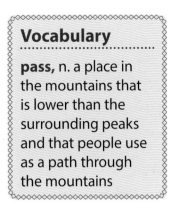
Athens and Sparta put aside their disagreements and united against the Persians. They were joined by a few other city-states. The Greeks had between two hundred and three hundred ships and an army of ten thousand men. The army was led by King Leonidas (/lee*ahn*uh*dus/) of Sparta.

The Greeks realized that the longer they could put off a major battle, the better their chances would be. The Greeks decided to delay the Persian army by engaging them at a place called Thermopylae (/thur*mahp*uh*lee/), about seventy-five miles northwest of Athens. Thermopylae was a narrow **pass** between high cliffs and the sea. Because of the narrowness of the pass, the Greeks hoped that the Persians

King Leonidas and three hundred Spartans fought the Persian army at Thermopylae.

would be unable to use their entire army, and therefore the Greeks might be able to hold the pass.

Things did not turn out exactly as planned. Leonidas and his troops showed great courage and managed to hold the pass for two days, but a native of the area, a man by the name of Ephialtes (/eff*ee*awl*teez/), showed the Persians how to use a mountain path to slip around the Greeks. When Leonidas realized what had happened, he ordered the majority of the Greeks to retreat. He and three hundred Spartans stayed behind to hold back the Persian army. All three hundred Spartans died defending the pass.

Salamis

The heroism of the Spartan troops slowed the Persian army but did not stop it. Xerxes marched south to Athens and burned the city to the ground. Fortunately, most of the citizens had been warned of the Persian army's approach and had **evacuated**.

> **Vocabulary**
>
> **evacuate,** v. to leave a place in an organized way, in order to get away from danger

After burning Athens, the Persians were set to conquer all of southern Greece. Xerxes decided to lead with his navy. The two fleets clashed near an island called Salamis (/sal*uh*mihs/). The Persians had big ships, but the Greeks were more familiar with the waterways. The Athenian navy lured the Persian fleet into shallow, narrow waters between the mainland and the island of Salamis. There, the Greek ships rammed and sank the Persian ships. The Greeks had also filled their boats with soldiers, who attacked the men on board the Persian ships. These tactics enabled the Athenian navy to defeat the huge Persian fleet.

Based on ancient sources, this painting from the 1900s shows the Battle of Salamis between the Greeks and the Persians. The Greeks were victorious.

Stunned by this unexpected loss, Xerxes immediately left Greece and sailed home. The next year, 479 BCE, the Spartan general Pausanias (/paw*say*nee*us/) led the Greeks against the Persians in the battle of Plataea (/pluh*tee*uh/). Pausanias won the battle and drove the Persian army out of Greece forever.

Chapter 6
The Golden Age of Athens

Rise of the Athenian Empire The Greeks' victory in the Persian Wars allowed the Greek city-states to remain free and independent. After the Persian Wars, Athens and Sparta were the two leading Greek city-states.

The Big Question

What were some of the cultural achievements during the Golden Age of Athens?

The Spartans had fought bravely at Thermopylae. They led the army during the final victory at Plataea. The Athenians had triumphed against all odds at Marathon. They defeated the Persian fleet during the naval battle of Salamis.

Although they were greatly outnumbered by the Persians, the Athenians were victorious at the Battle of Marathon.

Athens and Sparta worked together during the war. But as soon as the war was over, they took separate paths. The Spartans went home to keep an eye on the helots. Meanwhile, Athens began building a mighty empire.

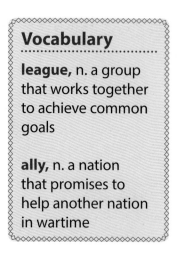
At the end of the war, many of the Greek city-states feared that the Persians might try to invade again. They wanted to form a **league** to defend themselves against such an invasion. In 478 BCE, they set up an alliance known as the Delian (/dee*lee*un/) League. Sparta did not participate in the Delian League, so Athens became the leader of the alliance.

Each of the city-states in the Delian League—named after the island of Delos in the middle of the Aegean Sea, where the league met—agreed to send money or ships to support the league. Athens decided how much money and how many ships each city-state had to send. Over time, Athens began treating the other members of the league less like **allies** and more like colonial subjects. Other city-states were made to swear a loyalty oath to Athens. They were not allowed to resign from the league.

Income from the Delian League helped fund what is now known as the Golden Age of Athens. The Golden Age lasted seventy-five years, from the end of the Persian Wars in 479 BCE until the end of the Peloponnesian (/pell*uh*pen*ee*shun/) War in 404 BCE. During this time, Athens produced some of the greatest artistic and cultural achievements the world has ever known.

Pericles

One important citizen of Athens during its Golden Age was Pericles (495–429 BCE). For nearly thirty years, Pericles (/pehr*ih*kleez/) was reelected again and again as one of the ten *strategoi,* or generals. Eventually, he became the most powerful and influential man in Athens.

One key to Pericles's success was his skill as an **orator**, or public speaker. One biographer said that his words were "like thunder and lightning." When Pericles proposed a measure, the Assembly usually

went along with him. Even though Pericles was technically only one citizen among many, he soon emerged as the leader of the Athenian city-state.

Pericles was well known for his hard work and dedication. It was said that he was never seen walking on any road besides the ones that led to government buildings. He did not believe in wasting time at parties and social events. He was rumored to have attended only one party during his lifetime and then he left early.

Under Pericles, the Athenian empire grew stronger. Pericles led armies in victorious campaigns. He helped keep the other members of the Delian League in line. He supervised the establishment of a number of Athenian colonies. He also convinced the Assembly to build bigger and stronger walls to protect Athens from attack. Walls stretched from Athens to the nearby seaport of Piraeus (/pye*ree*us/). Without these walls, an attacking army could surround the city and cut off its food supplies. With the walls, it would be possible for the Athenian navy to bring in food supplies from overseas, even while the enemy attacked. (This was why Athens had to have a powerful navy.)

Athens reached its greatest height of accomplishments under the leadership of Pericles.

Pericles also strengthened Athenian democracy. Before Pericles, poor Athenians were often unable to participate in government. As citizens, they had the right to do so. However, because government work (including being part of a jury) did not pay, a poor citizen often could not afford to leave his paying job to accept an unpaid government position. Pericles convinced the Athenians to pay citizens for government work. This opened the Athenian democracy to a wider range of citizens.

Pericles is also remembered as a supporter of the arts. He supported **dramatists**, painters, sculptors, and **architects**. In 449 BCE, Pericles suggested that Athens rebuild the temples and public buildings in the Acropolis, a complex of buildings on a bluff overlooking the city. The temples and buildings on the Athenians' Acropolis had been destroyed during the Persian Wars. Rebuilding it would be

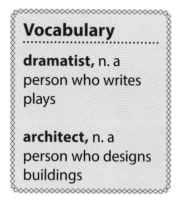

Vocabulary

dramatist, n. a person who writes plays

architect, n. a person who designs buildings

expensive, but Pericles had a plan. He said the Athenians could take some of the money they were getting from their allies in the Delian League and spend it on this important architectural project.

This idea was controversial. Many of the members of the Delian League complained that it was unfair to use their money to beautify Athens. Even some Athenians questioned the strategy. Pericles used Athenian military power to make the other Greek city-states accept his plan. He used his oratorical skills to convince the Athenians that his plan was acceptable. Pericles said that as long as Athens was protecting its allies, it could use the excess money in any way it saw fit.

The Parthenon

The most famous of all the buildings built under Pericles's leadership was the Parthenon (/par*thuh*non/). The Parthenon is a temple to Athena (/uh*theen*uh/), the Greek goddess of wisdom, for whom the city of Athens was named. Built between 447 and 432 BCE, the Parthenon is considered the greatest of all Greek buildings and one of the treasures of human culture. It was badly damaged by an explosion in the late 1600s, when it was being used to store gunpowder during a war. However, the Parthenon still stands. It is 2,500 years old. Thousands of tourists travel to Athens each year to see it.

The image above shows the Parthenon as it is today. The structure was built on a hill so that it could be seen from miles away. The Parthenon was the spiritual center of ancient Greece and was built to honor the goddess Athena.

Believe it or not, there is a reconstruction of the Parthenon in Nashville, Tennessee. You can see it in this image, set against the modern buildings of downtown Nashville.

Pericles recruited two leading architects to design and build the Parthenon. He wanted them to build a temple that would honor Athena but would also serve as a symbol of the wealth, power, and prosperity of Athens. They did not let him down. The two designed a rectangular building larger than any other temple on the mainland of Greece. It was roughly 230 feet long, 100 feet wide, and 60 feet high. More than twenty thousand tons of marble were used in the construction process.

The architects placed a colonnade, or row of columns, on each of the four sides of the building. Many Greek architects before them had used this same technique. Indeed, the Greeks were so fond of columns that they eventually developed three styles of architecture, each of which was based on a distinctive kind of column. These three styles, or orders, were called Doric, Ionic, and Corinthian.

The Doric (/dawr*ihk/) column was the oldest and simplest of the three. It featured a large ridged column with a capital, or top, shaped like a saucer. The Ionic (/eye*ahn*ihk/) style of column was tall and slender with spiral scroll-like curlicues on either side of the capital. The Corinthian (/kuh*rihn*thee*un/)

Greek Columns

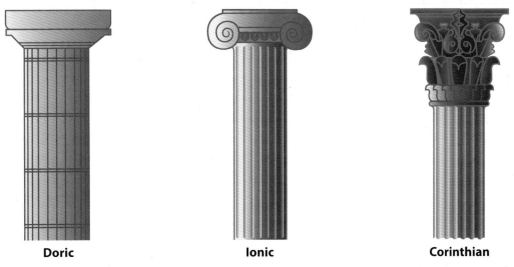

| Doric | Ionic | Corinthian |

The ancient Greeks used three different styles of columns for their buildings.

column was the most ornate. The capital on top of a Corinthian column looks like a basket with layers of leaves in it.

The architects used Doric columns for the Parthenon, which is now widely considered to be one of the finest examples of Doric architecture ever built. The carvings on the sides of the temple were done by an artist named Pheidias (/fihd*ee*us/), the most famous sculptor of ancient Greece. He worked with his students and builders from all over Greece to create them. The carvings depicted religious ceremonies and mythological battles between gods and mortals.

Inside the temple the ceiling was high enough to hold a forty-foot-tall statue of Athena. This statue, also made by Pheidias, was covered with ivory and gold. The ivory was used for the skin of the goddess and the gold for her clothing. The statue cost even more than the building that housed it. Unfortunately, it was destroyed in ancient times, though a small copy has survived.

Greek Drama

Athenian architects also built large outdoor theaters for dramatic performances. The most important Athenian theater was the Theater of Dionysus (/dye*uh*nye*sus/), located below the Acropolis, not far from the Parthenon. In this semicircular, open-air theater, fifteen thousand Athenians gathered.

Like the Olympics, Greek drama began as part of a religious festival. In this case it was a festival in honor of the Greek god of wine, Dionysus. At first a chorus of men danced around the altar of Dionysus, singing in honor of the god. Gradually, performances became more complex. At first a single actor was introduced in addition to the chorus; then additional actors were included, to allow for conversation and discussion among actors. Eventually, Greek drama began to look a lot like what we think of as a play.

Just as Greek athletes were given prizes for athletic excellence at the Olympics, so Athenian playwrights were given prizes for excellence in the

Greek theaters were designed so that even a whisper on stage could be heard from every seat. Today, modern audiences still respond to the plays of ancient Greece. Here you can see the ruins of the Theater of Dionysus.

Theater of Dionysus. Each year several dramatists would present plays, and a panel of judges would give prizes for the best plays.

The performances were paid for by wealthy men like Pericles. The actors were Athenian citizens. It seems that many Athenian citizens served their city not only in government but also on the stage. According to one estimate, as many as three thousand citizens performed in the festival each year.

The Athenian dramatists invented two kinds of drama that are still important today: comedy and tragedy. Comedies were funny plays with happy endings. They often addressed contemporary issues. The most famous comic playwright was Aristophanes (/ar*ih*stahf*uh*neez/). Tragedies, on the other hand, were serious plays with sad endings. They were usually based on well-known Greek myths. The most famous tragic playwrights were Aeschylus (/es*kih*lus/), Sophocles (/sohf*uh*kleez/), and Euripides (/yoo*rihp*uh*deez/).

The Big Four

Aeschylus, who was born around 525 BCE, was the oldest of the four major Athenian dramatists. He was old enough to have fought against the Persians. When the Persian Wars were over, he became the leading dramatist of his day. In 472 BCE, Aeschylus wrote a play about the Persian Wars. This play was sponsored by Pericles himself. Later, Aeschylus wrote a famous three-part play called the *Oresteia* (/awr*es*tye*uh/), about murders and revenge. According to legend, one scene completely terrified the audience in the Theater of Dionysus. Aeschylus wrote more than eighty plays in total. Unfortunately, only seven of these plays have survived.

Sophocles was thirty years younger than Aeschylus. When Aeschylus and the Athenian navy defeated the Persians at Salamis, Sophocles was only a teenager. However, because of his boyish good looks and dramatic skills, he was chosen to play a leading role in a dramatic performance celebrating the victory. Later, Sophocles began writing plays. He and Aeschylus became dramatic rivals. They competed for top honors during the festivals of Dionysus. Sophocles also played a role in public affairs. Sophocles's most famous play is called *Oedipus the King*.

The last of the great tragic playwrights was Euripides. He was born around 485 BCE. Euripides produced eighty or ninety plays. Although he won fewer prizes than Aeschylus and Sophocles, he was popular with Athenian audiences. He is widely admired today for his analysis of human nature.

Marble bust of Sophocles

The great master of Athenian comedy was Aristophanes, who lived from 445 to around 380 BCE. In his plays, Aristophanes made fun of **statesmen** like Pericles, dramatists like Euripides,

Vocabulary

statesman, n. a political leader

and philosophers like Socrates (/sahk*ruh*teez/), whom you will meet in Chapter 8.

Athenian drama was an astonishing achievement. The plays are so powerful and so well written that they are still admired and performed today.

Other Cultural Achievements

In addition to architecture and drama, many other arts also flourished during the Golden Age of Athens.

Athenian craftsmen produced distinctive pottery, including bowls, urns, and vases. Much of this pottery was decorated with pictures. The pictures showed episodes from mythology, religious rites, Olympic competitions, and everyday scenes. These decorated urns and vases were used to hold oils, foods, and beverages. They were sold all around the Greek world and beyond. Today, they are even more valuable than they were in the Golden Age. Museums display them for the beautiful scenes they show, and scholars use them to learn about everyday life in ancient Athens.

This age also gave the world two of its first historians. Herodotus (/huh*rod*uh*tus/) is often called the father of history. He wrote down the history of the Persian Wars, including the last stand at Thermopylae. Thucydides (/thoo*sihd*ih*deez/) told the story of the Peloponnesian War, which you will read about in the next chapter.

There were also advances in science and medicine. The famous doctor, Hippocrates (/hih*pahk*ruh*teez/), is considered the father of medicine. Hippocrates, who was born around 460 BCE, was one of the first to recognize that weather, drinking water, and location can influence people's health. He is chiefly remembered for the Hippocratic (/hihp*uh*krat*ihk/) oath, a pledge that doctors have been taking for almost 2,500 years. When new doctors recite the Hippocratic oath, they agree to use their medical skills only for the good of the patient: "I do solemnly swear . . . that into whatsoever house I shall enter, it shall be for the good of the sick."

Pericles was very proud of Athenian culture. He described the city as "an education for Greece," and not only for Greece, but for all time. When one considers all the achievements of this era—beautiful temples and theaters, raucous comedies and heartbreaking tragedies, stylish vases and urns, groundbreaking historical writings, and important medical advances—it is hard not to agree. The Golden Age of Athens was truly one of the greatest periods in the history of human culture.

Amphoras often had lids, such as the one here. This urn is from the 300s BCE and shows a wedding scene.

Chapter 7
The Peloponnesian War

Athens versus Sparta Sparta watched with concern as Athens built its empire. The Spartans worried that Athens was becoming too powerful. They also resented Athenian attempts to push Athenian-style democracy onto other Greek city-states.

The Big Question

What events brought about an end to the Golden Age of Athens?

Here you can see the ruins of the ancient city of Corinth. The columns of the Apollo Temple are still standing.

Sparta and several of its allies, including the city-states of Corinth and Thebes, came together to form the Peloponnesian League. This league was named for the Peloponnesus (/pel*uh*puh*nee*sus/), a mountainous peninsula that forms the southern part of Greece. Sparta and several of its allies were located on the Peloponnesus.

During the 430s BCE, **diplomatic relations** between Athens and the Peloponnesian League worsened. In 431 BCE, the Peloponnesian War broke out. This devastating war continued for more than twenty-five years and eventually put an end to the Athenian empire.

Beginning of the War

When the war began, Pericles was still the leader of Athens. He knew that the Spartan army was stronger than the Athenian army. He also knew that Athens had a stronger navy and was far wealthier. Pericles believed that if the Athenians could avoid a major land battle, they had a good chance of winning.

Pericles developed a plan. He decided that the Spartans probably wanted a quick victory and not a slow, lengthy war. So Athens would refuse to meet the Spartan army in a land battle in which the Athenians would probably be defeated. While the Spartans were trying to make them fight, the Athenians would stay behind the walls they had built. Meanwhile, the Athenians would use their navy to bring supplies to Athens and to attack towns along the coast of the Peloponnesus.

Pericles convinced the citizens of Athens to follow his plan. All the farmers who lived in the area around Athens were told to leave their farms and take refuge in the city. The country people poured into the city, bringing with them their wives, their children, and their most valuable belongings. The historian Thucydides reported that many of them brought not only their furniture but also their doors and their window shutters!

When the Spartans marched on Athens, they found a deserted countryside. They burned the farmhouses and the crops in the fields. They did this to lure the Athenians into battle. A battle the Spartans believed they could win.

The Athenians could see the smoke from the fires. They begged Pericles to let them fight. But the cautious Pericles thought fighting would be too dangerous. The

Pericles believed it was safer to stay inside the city walls than to fight the Spartans on the battlefield.

crops would grow back, Pericles told the Athenians, but "dead men will not." Pericles had decided on a waiting game. He figured the longer the Spartans had to wait for the Athenians to come out and fight, the fewer supplies they would have.

During the first year of the war, this strategy succeeded. Because they had burned the fields, the Spartans could not find any food. Finally, the Spartan army gave up and left. By the time they made it home, the Athenian navy had attacked several of the coastal cities of the Peloponnesus.

The War Continues

The second year of the war began with another Spartan land attack. Once again, the Athenian people retreated behind their walls. This time, however, things did not turn out so well for the Athenians. A deadly **plague** swept through the city, killing nearly a quarter of the population.

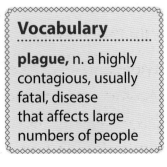

Vocabulary

plague, n. a highly contagious, usually fatal, disease that affects large numbers of people

The plague lasted for three years. It was so terrible that the people of Athens became deeply discouraged. They wondered whether the gods had turned against them. Life and property became cheap. People no longer felt that honesty, truth, and justice had any meaning since they thought they might die the next day. Worst of all, Pericles died in the plague and was replaced by men who were not as wise as he had been.

The war dragged on for years with no victory for either side. As long as the Athenian army would not fight the Spartan army, the Spartans could not win. As long as the Athenian navy only made random raids on the Peloponnesian cities, the Athenians could not win. Something had to be done.

About 415 BCE, an Athenian named Alcibiades (/al*suh*bye*uh*deez/) proposed that the Athenians conquer the island of Sicily, now a part of Italy but then inhabited by Greeks. This island was on the other side of the Peloponnesus. If it was conquered, then Athens could renew its supplies, attack Sparta from both sides, and defeat their archrivals. Some Athenian citizens liked the idea. It was bold and daring. A few were not so sure. They didn't feel they had the military strength to conquer Sicily and carry on a war with Sparta and its allies at the same time. They also distrusted Alcibiades. He was a very charming young man, but he drank and gambled. He also showed a lack of respect for many of the traditions and ideals of the Athenians.

Still, enough Athenian citizens liked the idea that the decision was made to invade Sicily and capture the main city of Syracuse. The invasion was a disaster. The invading Athenian army met strong resistance. They held out for as long as they could, but finally tried to escape in a panic. The army was divided, many were killed, and still others were taken captive and enslaved in the **rock quarries** in Sicily. They lived out the rest of their lives in misery, far away from their democracy in Athens.

Alcibiades was ordered to return to Athens just as the invasion forces arrived in Sicily. But he decided

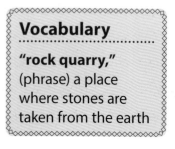

Vocabulary

"rock quarry," (phrase) a place where stones are taken from the earth

to flee to Sparta instead. There, he told the Spartans of Athens's plans. He was willing to be a traitor in order to save his own life. The Spartans took the information but did not trust him. Alcibiades realized that the Spartans might kill him, so he fled once more. This time he went to Persia. But even there it was clear that he was not a man who could be trusted.

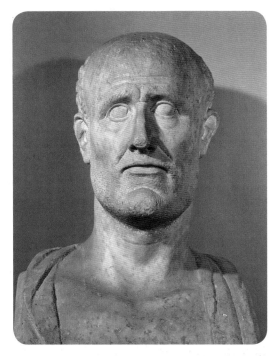

This is a Greek marble sculpture of Alcibiades.

The Sicilian disaster tilted the balance of power in favor of Sparta. The Athenian army and navy had been seriously weakened by the losses in Sicily. Now, the Spartans began to build a navy of their own. They also enlisted the Persians as allies. In 405 BCE, the Spartans scored a major naval victory. This enabled them to cut off grain supplies to Athens. Athens held out as long as it could, but in 404 BCE, the city surrendered. The Spartans and their allies had won the Peloponnesian War.

The Spartans made the Athenians tear down the walls that had protected their city. They prohibited Athens from having a navy, and they set up the government they wanted Athens to have. The city-state would now be ruled by a group of thirty nobles—members of the upper class. There would be no more democracy.

However, the nobles were so corrupt and cruel that within a year, the Athenians rebelled against them. In 403 BCE, democracy was restored. The kings of Sparta decided that as long as Athens was peaceful, they would let Athenian citizens have their democracy. But the Athenian empire and the Golden Age of Athens were over.

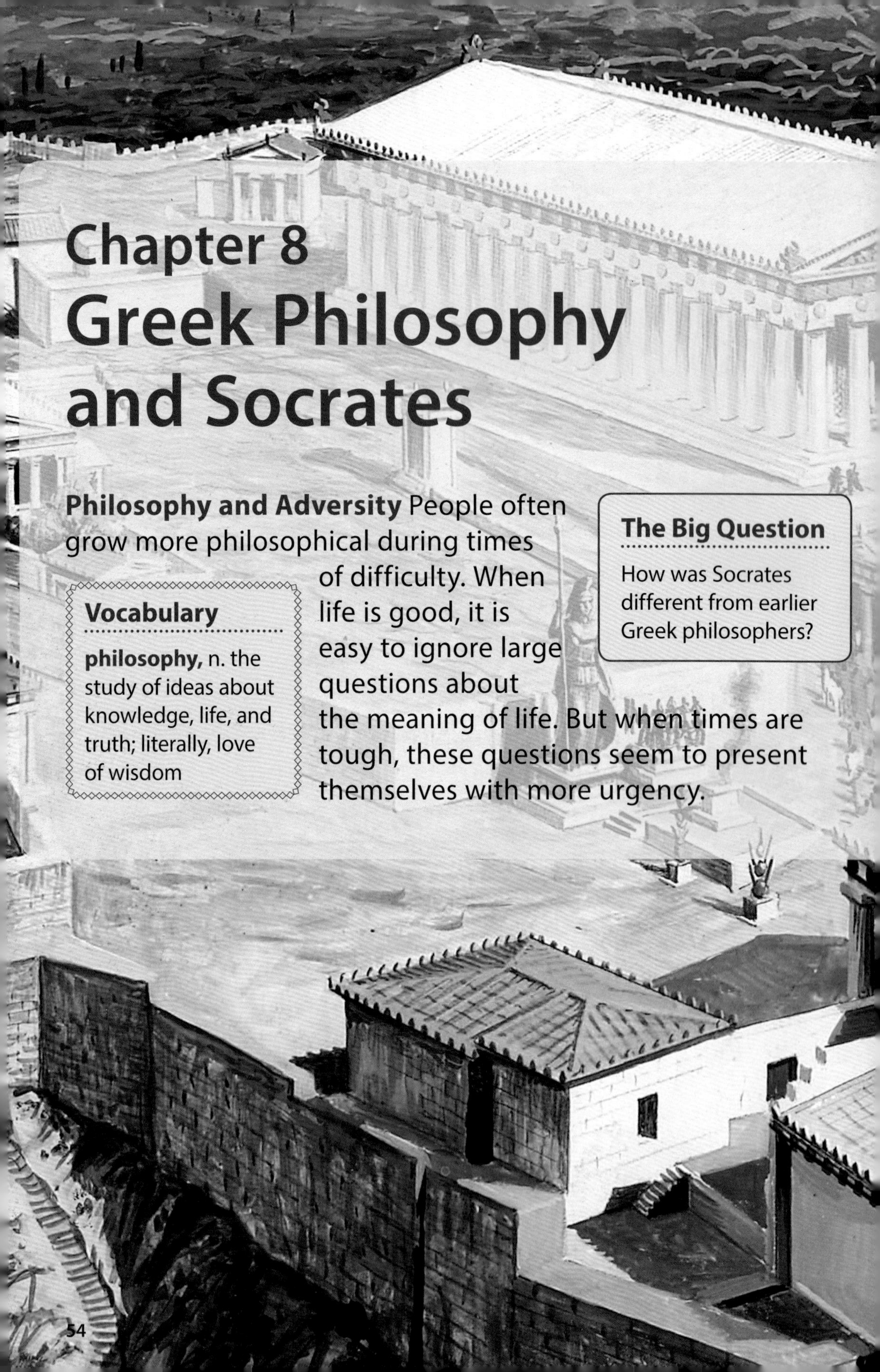

Chapter 8
Greek Philosophy and Socrates

Philosophy and Adversity People often grow more philosophical during times of difficulty. When life is good, it is easy to ignore large questions about the meaning of life. But when times are tough, these questions seem to present themselves with more urgency.

Vocabulary

philosophy, n. the study of ideas about knowledge, life, and truth; literally, love of wisdom

The Big Question

How was Socrates different from earlier Greek philosophers?

The Parthenon sits on a hill above the modern city of Athens.

In these images, you can see an artist's impression of the city of Athens as it once was, and a photograph of what part of the city looks like today.

55

The history of Athens seems to demonstrate this point. As the Athenian empire collapsed, Athenian philosophy burst into magnificent bloom. During the last years of the Peloponnesian War and the decades that followed, Athens fell on hard times militarily and politically. Yet the city-state was home to a string of brilliant and influential philosophers, including Socrates, Plato (/play*toh/), and Aristotle (/ar*ess*taht*ul/).

Early Greek Philosophy

Of course, some Greeks had asked philosophical questions before these three philosophers came along. In earlier times they had asked questions such as: How can we understand the world around us? Where did the earth come from? How did the universe get started? Why is life so full of troubles? Like people in other ancient cultures, the Greeks told stories that helped them understand the world. They said that natural events were caused by the gods. A storm at sea meant that the sea god Poseidon was angry. A thunderstorm meant that Zeus was throwing his thunderbolt spear. The world was full of troubles because Zeus had given the first woman, Pandora, a jar or box, with strict instructions that she not open it. But Pandora's curiosity got the better of her. She opened the lid, releasing all the evils and miseries that hurt humanity.

By the 500s BCE, however, some people were no longer satisfied with the answers given by the myths. Some of them no longer believed that gods and goddesses were behind natural **phenomena**. They wondered whether there weren't other ways to understand the world. Eventually, some Greeks began to use **reason** to try to understand the world. This was the beginning of philosophy.

> ## Vocabulary
>
> **phenomena,** n. observable events; in nature, occurrences such as sun, rain, storms, and earthquakes
>
> **reason,** n. the ability of the mind to think and understand

A philosopher is a person who uses reason to try to acquire wisdom about life or the universe. Many of the early Greek philosophers tried to figure out where the world came from, how it began, and what it was made of. Some of their ideas have stood the test of time and are still considered important. Other ideas seem strange to us today. But at least the early philosophers were trying to figure things out by using their brains.

The early philosopher Heraclitus (/her*ah*klite*us/) held that everything in life is always changing. It is impossible, Heraclitus said, to step in the same river twice, because the river itself is always flowing and never at rest. This is an idea that still makes sense to us today. But Heraclitus also seems to have thought that to live long, it was important

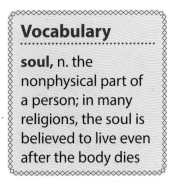

to keep one's **soul** from becoming too wet. At death, a dry soul would rise all the way to the sun and help bring about light, day, and summer. But a wet soul would only rise as far as the moon, where it would help bring about winter, night, and rain. These ideas make less sense to us.

Another early philosopher, Thales (/thay*leez/) taught that everything in the universe comes from water. The philosopher Anaximenes (/an*ak*sihm*uh*neez/) believed that everything comes from air. Air is alive with movement, he reasoned, and so air must be the origin of all life. Empedocles (/em*ped*uh*kleez/) had a slightly more complicated theory. He proposed that everything comes from the combination or separation of four elements: earth, air, fire, and water.

Some of these theories or ideas came from simple observation of the world in which they lived. It took a long time before

Heraclitus

philosophers began to test their ideas. Still, these early philosophers were important because they were attempting to answer difficult questions. They were teaching themselves and their listeners how to reason, instead of just accepting the old myths.

Socrates

One of the most famous of all the Greek philosophers and teachers was an Athenian named Socrates, who lived from 469 BCE to 399 BCE. Socrates grew up during the Golden Age of Athens but lived to see that Golden Age crumble during the Peloponnesian War, in which he fought. Most of what we know about the philosophical ideas of Socrates comes from the writings of one of his students, named Plato. Socrates himself wrote nothing. Yet, because he was immortalized in the writings of Plato, when we think of Greek philosophy, we always think of Socrates.

Socrates was different from earlier Greek philosophers in several ways. First of all, he was more interested in questions about how human beings should behave than about where the world came from or what it might be made of. Socrates was one of the first philosophers to study **ethics**.

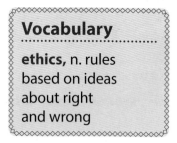

Vocabulary

ethics, n. rules based on ideas about right and wrong

Socrates also had some unusual methods of philosophizing. Instead of just sitting in his room and writing about philosophical questions, he went to the Athenian marketplace, called the *agora,* and talked with other Athenians. In this way, Socrates made philosophy personal.

During his discussions, Socrates tried to get the Athenians to examine their lives. He wanted them to realize that they were not

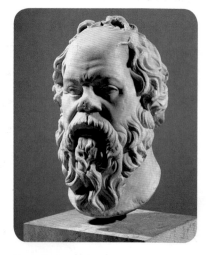

Socrates

The agora was the heart of Athenian economy and social life. Socrates enjoyed talking to the people of Athens there.

always living according to the ideals and values they said were important. He tried to convince Athenians that "the unexamined life is not worth living."

He tried to get them to understand this by asking them questions, instead of giving direct answers. Socrates would ask his listeners to explain what they meant by an important concept or idea, such as justice. Then he would point out the contradictions between what they said and how they lived. By doing this, he was not trying to condemn people as **hypocrites**. He was trying to get people to think more deeply about their lives and about moral and ethical ideals.

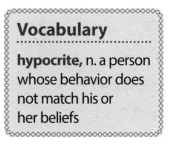

Vocabulary

hypocrite, n. a person whose behavior does not match his or her beliefs

The Socratic Method

We can get an idea of what Socrates might have sounded like by looking at an excerpt from Plato's works. In the following passage, Socrates is talking with a friend named Crito, making a comparison between physical fitness and moral or ethical fitness:

> SOCRATES: Well, is life worth living with a body which is worn out and ruined in health?
>
> CRITO: Certainly not.
>
> SOCRATES: What about the part of us which is mutilated by wrong actions and benefited by right ones? Is life worth living with this part ruined? Or do we believe that this part of us, whatever it may be, in which right and wrong operate, is of less importance than the body?
>
> CRITO: Certainly not.
>
> SOCRATES: Is it really more precious?
>
> CRITO: Much more.
>
> SOCRATES: In that case, my dear fellow, what we ought to consider is not so much what people in general will say about us but how we stand with the expert in right and wrong, the one authority, who represents the actual truth.

We cannot be certain that these are Socrates's exact words. The words were written down later by Plato. But we do know that this was the way Socrates worked, by asking a series of questions that were designed to lead the listeners to realizations about how they ought to behave.

Today, this question-asking method is known as the *Socratic method*. It is still widely used. Whenever your teacher asks you a series of questions, trying to get you to realize or understand something, he or she is using the Socratic method.

Unlike other Greek teachers, called **sophists**, who were paid for their words of wisdom, Socrates did not receive money for teaching. He did not want money for his ideas. He did not care about

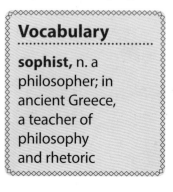

Vocabulary

sophist, n. a philosopher; in ancient Greece, a teacher of philosophy and rhetoric

personal comforts. Once when he was passing through the marketplace, he remarked, "How many things I can do without!"

Socrates also differed from the teachers of his day by claiming that he did not have wisdom. He questioned people who claimed to be wise, in order to find out what made them wise (or gave them the reputation for wisdom), and constantly found that they claimed to know things—but really did not. He said he himself was wise only in *one* thing: he at least knew that he knew nothing.

Socrates insisted that he had never taught anyone anything. He simply liked to have conversations. His conversations, however, were always based on two principles. Socrates believed strongly that it was important never to do any wrong, even indirectly. The second principle was that people who really understood what was right and good could not possibly choose the wrong thing.

Although some people liked Socrates, many others found him very annoying. Socrates was constantly talking and expressing his ideas, even when these ideas were unpopular. Socrates also got on people's nerves by pointing out their faults. Nobody likes to be reminded of their shortcomings, especially when they are in front of others. Eventually, Socrates was arrested on the charge of corrupting, or harming, the young men of Athens.

Some of the citizens of Athens felt that Socrates had misled the young men of the city. They accused the philosopher of failing to teach the young proper respect for older people and for the gods. They said he encouraged young men to be selfish and power hungry. Alcibiades had been one of Socrates's favorite students, they said. Other students had been involved in the corrupt government that ruled Athens at the end of the Peloponnesian War. Some Athenians held Socrates responsible for the way these young men had treated the rest of the citizens of Athens.

The Death of Socrates

Plato wrote a series of works about the last days of Socrates. One of these works describes the trial in which Socrates defended himself but was eventually convicted (by a vote of 280 to 221) and sentenced to death.

Plato also wrote down conversations that Socrates had with his friends while he was in prison awaiting death. When someone suggested that there were important people who would help Socrates escape from prison, the philosopher refused to save himself and rejected their help. He argued, "One must obey the commands of one's city and country, or persuade it as to the nature of justice." Socrates refused to break the law, even when it condemned him. The citizens of Athens had condemned him to death, and he would face death because it was the right thing to do. He would not put himself above the law.

This painting is called *The Death of Socrates*. It was painted by Jacques-Louis David, a French artist, in the 1700s.

Socrates was executed by being made to drink hemlock, a kind of poison. Plato described Socrates continuing to talk with his friends after he drank the hemlock before gradually drifting into death. In reality, the death of Socrates must have been much more gruesome. Plato chose not to focus on his death but rather on the fact that Socrates was an example of reason and self-control right up to the bitter end. He wanted Socrates to be remembered as Plato himself remembered him, as "a man of whom we may say that of all whom we met at that time he was the wisest and most just and best."

Today, Socrates is remembered for the Socratic method and for his commitment to seeking truth. He expanded the role of the philosopher to include the important task of examining how people live their lives. It wasn't enough for Socrates to think about what goodness meant ideally. He wanted people to choose goodness and live rightly every day. That is why his contributions to philosophy are still important to us all these centuries later.

Chapter 9
Plato and Aristotle

Plato Like Socrates, Plato was born in Athens and spent his life as a philosopher searching for truth. Plato was not only a brilliant thinker but also a brilliant writer. He wrote down many of his ideas, and his **dialogues** are still widely read today.

The Big Question

What role did philosophers play in ancient Greece, and what were their long-term contributions?

Vocabulary

dialogue, n. a piece of writing organized as a conversation between two or more characters

Plato was about twenty-four when the Peloponnesian War ended. When Socrates was executed, Plato fled Athens with other students of Socrates. Because their teacher had been executed, they felt that they were not welcome in Athens.

Plato traveled from place to place for a number of years. He even visited Italy and Sicily. Eventually, he returned to Athens. In 387 BCE, he started a school called the Academy. This school lasted more than nine hundred years, until the Roman emperor Justinian, who reigned from 527–565 CE, closed it because it did not teach Christianity.

Plato's Academy was a center for philosophical and intellectual thought. It lasted for hundreds of years.

The Dialogues

In some of his early dialogues, Plato tried to write down conversations that Socrates had actually had with others. He wanted to let people know what Socrates had said. In his later dialogues, Plato still used the dialogue form but used it to treat new subjects. These dialogues were not necessarily based on things Socrates had actually said. Rather, Plato tried to imagine what his beloved teacher Socrates *might* have said about various subjects.

By writing dialogues, Plato allowed his readers to imagine that they were part of a great philosophical conversation. He encouraged them to think about their own opinions and ideas, and he showed them that they could use reason to discover truth.

Although Plato wrote Socratic dialogues, his way of searching for truth and trying to understand goodness differed from the methods used by Socrates. Plato was more **idealistic** than his teacher. He spent more time trying to understand what the ideal, or perfect example, of goodness

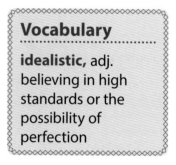

Vocabulary
....
idealistic, adj.
believing in high
standards or the
possibility of
perfection

was and less time trying to help people recognize whether they were actually living it. Plato was also more traditional in his teaching methods. He didn't confront people in the street or marketplace. Like many other philosophers, he had regular students whom he taught. However, before people could study with Plato, they had to have mastered mathematics.

Plato felt that philosophers should play the central role in society because they alone understood the meaning of truth and justice. He did not believe in democracy. He thought it gave power to people who did not understand justice—people who did wicked things, such as execute Socrates.

Plato wanted society to be like a school, in which citizens spent their lives training to be good people (just as in Sparta they trained to be good soldiers). He imagined an ideal state, ruled by philosophers and dedicated to justice.

Here, citizens could develop **virtue** within themselves and choose goodness. Plato believed that the right kind of education would teach citizens to control themselves, to act for the good of others,

and to be less selfish. His long dialogue, *The Republic,* describes his ideal state.

During the lifetime of Socrates, philosophers were involved in the life of the polis. They tried to educate citizens and get them involved. By the time

Plato encouraged people to use reason to find answers.

Plato was teaching and writing, things had changed. The role of the philosopher was still to train citizens, but it was also important for a philosopher to use his knowledge to point out how society was not always what it could be. Philosophers taught in schools rather than conversing in the marketplace or debating in the Assembly. They tried to identify what was wrong with society and made suggestions for how it could be better. However, they were not directly involved in the everyday life of the polis as earlier philosophers had been. When the great philosopher Aristotle came along, he made even more changes in what philosophers did and how they worked.

Aristotle

Just as Socrates found a great student in Plato, so Plato found a great student in Aristotle. Aristotle was born around 384 BCE in Macedonia, a country north of Greece. There, his father had been a doctor in the court of the king, Amyntas III. When Aristotle came to Athens, he studied with Plato and stayed at Plato's school for twenty years before starting his own school, called the Lyceum (/lye*see*um/).

Aristotle was greatly influenced both by his father and by Plato. His father had influenced him because, in ancient times, knowledge and skills were passed from father to son. Aristotle's father was a doctor. As a doctor, he had to take careful note of a patient's symptoms, or signs of illness, to understand what was making a patient sick. He taught Aristotle to observe people and the world around him carefully.

Plato taught Aristotle how important **abstract** ideals and knowledge are. Aristotle and Plato disagreed and argued with each other from time to time. Aristotle admired Plato greatly, but he once said, "Plato is dear to me, but dearer still is truth."

> ### Vocabulary
>
> **abstract,** adj.
> relating to ideas, rather than concrete objects, actions, or people

Plato and Aristotle are the central figures in this painting, called *The School of Athens*. It was painted by the Italian Renaissance artist Raphael.

A Keen Observer

Aristotle also added to the knowledge of his day by collecting and examining insects, animals, and plants. He loved to study animals. He dissected more than fifty different types of animals in order to learn about them.

From his years of careful observation, Aristotle realized that there is always more than one way to explain things. For example, an animal could be understood by what it looked like, what it was made of, how it moved, and what it could do. All these different explanations were important and necessary.

Aristotle didn't know it, but by collecting facts, analyzing them, and coming up with theories about his observations, he was developing the basics of scientific research. It's true that Aristotle didn't go as far as later philosophers did in testing out his ideas. Some of his ideas turned out to be wrong. However, he helped move philosophy down the path that would eventually lead to modern science.

Like other philosophers, Aristotle also wrote about what it meant to lead a good and just life. He believed that the purpose of life was to exercise one's abilities and virtues reasonably. In his book *Nicomachean* (/nihk*oh*mak*ee*un/)

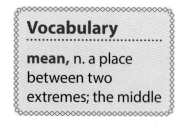

Vocabulary

mean, n. a place between two extremes; the middle

Ethics, he said, "Virtue, therefore, is a kind of moderation or **mean** as it aims at the mean or moderate amount." Aristotle meant that people should avoid extremes of all kinds. Just as they should eat neither too much nor too little, so they should avoid both evil deeds on the one hand and self-righteousness on the other. Aristotle believed that a truly virtuous man is neither cowardly nor foolishly brave. Aristotle wrote, "It is possible to feel fear, confidence, desire, anger, pity—but to feel these emotions at the right times, on the right occasions, and toward the right people in the right ways is the best course." This idea of living moderately is sometimes called "the golden mean."

Aristotle also examined politics, or the life of the state. He was interested in determining the best kinds of governments. He wanted to identify which types of governments care for the citizens and not just the rulers. So he inspected dozens of city-states. In his book, *The Politics,* Aristotle wrote that the purpose of the state was to make "the good life" possible for its citizens. The state should create a society in which people could live nobly, honorably, and well.

A Man of His Time

Aristotle was a man of his time, however, and he did not believe that all people were equal. He valued men above women. He believed that aristocrats were morally superior to non-aristocrats. He also believed in slavery. He felt that an enslaved person was the property of the slave owner just as a tool was his property.

Aristotle's influence lasted for centuries. During the European Middle Ages, he was so important that he was referred to simply as "the Philosopher."

The great Athenian philosophers, Socrates, Plato, and Aristotle, taught each other to use reason to examine their lives, society, and the world around them. Much of what we know and think about today is based on the principles of reason and observation that began with these philosophers of ancient Greece.

Chapter 10
Alexander and the Hellenistic Period

Brave and Daring General During Aristotle's lifetime, a king named Alexander rose to great **prominence**. Some say he was the greatest general who ever lived. He certainly accomplished a great deal during his brief lifetime and changed the Mediterranean world forever.

Alexander conquered more land than anyone else before him had ever done. He also collected more wealth than anyone before him. And he ruled more people than any previous king. For these reasons, we call him Alexander the Great.

Alexander had been one of Aristotle's students. His father was Philip II, the king of Macedonia. When Alexander was about twenty years old, his father was **assassinated**, and Alexander became king. Because he was so young, most people thought that Alexander would be easily removed from the throne by his father's enemies. But Alexander surprised everyone. He crushed those who wanted to get rid of him. Then he began to increase the size of his empire.

This image is of a Roman mosaic depicting Alexander the Great in battle.

Alexander was strong, handsome, and extremely intelligent. He was also a fearless fighter who never hesitated to put himself in the worst part of the battle. This made his troops very loyal to him. It also made his enemies afraid of him because they were never sure where his daring and courage would lead him.

As a young man, Alexander helped his father conquer Greece. (This was not hard to do because the Greek city-states were disorganized.) After his father's death, Alexander decided to attack Greece's old enemies, the Persians. In 334 BCE, the Persian Empire was still very large. It extended all the way to the shores of the Mediterranean Sea and included present-day Iran, Afghanistan, Turkey, the Middle East, and Egypt.

At the time, Alexander just had a small army of about thirty thousand **infantrymen** and another five thousand men on horseback. He had no navy. But Alexander didn't care. His plan was to gain a couple of quick and easy victories so that he would have supplies on hand. Then, people would want to follow him because he was brave and strong.

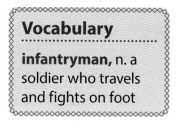

Vocabulary

infantryman, n. a soldier who travels and fights on foot

Alexander and the Persian Empire

Alexander and his army attacked Asia Minor and conquered it. He faced the Persian king Darius III in a battle and was so fierce that the king and the Persian army broke ranks and fled. This enabled Alexander to march south, seizing towns along the coast of the Mediterranean Sea. He conquered the Middle East, including the city of Jerusalem. He took over everything between Asia Minor and Egypt.

The Persian king asked Alexander for peace. He promised Alexander that he would not attack his army if Alexander let him keep the other half of his empire. Because Alexander had never lost a battle, he saw no reason to accept Darius III's offer. Alexander wanted all of the Persian Empire.

The Battle of Alexander at Issus, painted by the German artist Albrecht Altdorfer, shows Alexander the Great's successful victory in battle over the Persians.

This image is a detail from a mosaic found in the ancient Roman town of Pompeii. It shows the battle between Darius and Alexander at Issus.

Meanwhile, the nobles of the Persian Empire were not happy with Darius III. They thought he was a weak king and a coward. They decided to arrest Darius and take on Alexander themselves. Once they had arrested the king, however, they found out that Alexander was coming after them. The nobles murdered Darius III and prepared to fight Alexander.

It took Alexander only eleven years to establish his empire. He gave the name "Alexandria" to several of the cities that he founded.

Alexander was brave and strong, but so were the Persian nobles. They forced Alexander to fight them for three years. He had to fight from mountain stronghold to mountain stronghold in the eastern part of the Persian Empire. Every time he captured one fortress, there would be another one waiting for him. And as he moved east, the nobles gathered their troops to attack him from behind. In the end, however, Alexander won. He had conquered the Persian Empire, the largest and most powerful empire of its time.

Conqueror of the World

Although Alexander had already created an immense empire, he did not stop. He led his army farther east toward India. By 326 BCE, he and his army were trying to conquer the western part of India. After winning one especially difficult battle, Alexander's army decided they had had enough. They did not want to fight anymore. They were tired of years and years of war, and they knew that this enemy army was far stronger than they were. They had won one battle, but they had not yet faced the largest part of the enemy army.

In ancient times, one of the weapons used in war was the attack elephant. Elephants were used in battle to charge against the enemy and trample soldiers. The Indian army that Alexander and his men had successfully faced had used two hundred of these trained elephants in the battle. But they

Empire of Alexander the Great, 300 BCE

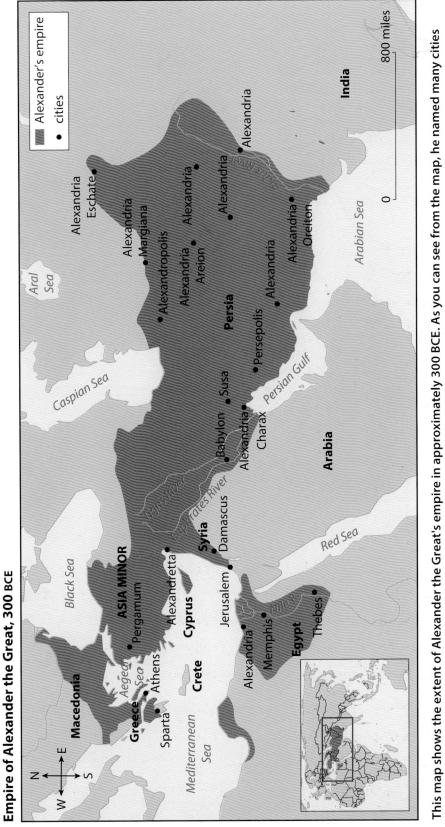

This map shows the extent of Alexander the Great's empire in approximately 300 BCE. As you can see from the map, he named many cities after himself.

knew that the Indian army had five thousand more elephants that they would have to defeat. Eventually, soldiers would learn how to sidestep or take down a charging elephant. But at this point in time, Alexander's men simply wanted to go home.

Having conquered what was then virtually all of the known world, Alexander returned to Babylon, a major city in Mesopotamia (present-day Iraq) and the center of his new empire. He was strong and capable, so the people of his empire probably expected that he would rule them for many years to come.

In 324 BCE, Alexander began to make plans for new projects, including establishing new cities. Unfortunately, it was not to be. In 323 BCE, Alexander caught a fever. Not long after, he died. He was only thirty-three years old.

Alexander was among the most brilliant and bravest military leaders the world has ever known. He never lost a battle and never gave up. Because of Alexander, the people who lived around the Mediterranean Sea came into contact with Greek culture. As a result, their ideas and knowledge changed forever.

Tales About Alexander

Whenever history produces a larger-than-life character, tales about that person spring up. Alexander the Great was no exception. Tall tales were repeated about him throughout the centuries. It was said that once when he wanted to cross the sea, the waves parted before him, showing the respect that even nature had for this extraordinary man.

Another tale concerned the Gordian knot. According to legend, Gordius, a king in Asia Minor, had tied a large complicated knot in a rope connected to a wagon he had dedicated to the god Zeus. It was said that the knot could only be undone by the man who was destined to rule Asia. Anyone who attempted to untie the knot and failed would be put to death. When

Alexander the Great saw the knot, he took out his sword, and with a single blow, cut it apart. Thus, Alexander the Great proved he was worthy to rule all of Asia. Today, the phrase "cutting the Gordian knot" is used when someone finds an unusual solution to a difficult problem.

The Hellenistic Period

Alexander the Great had a short life, but his accomplishments had a long-lasting impact. In the years after his death, Greek, or Hellenic, culture spread to many of the lands he had conquered. Because Greek culture was so important to so many people during these years, the period from the death of Alexander in 323 BCE to 30 BCE is often known as the **Hellenistic** Period.

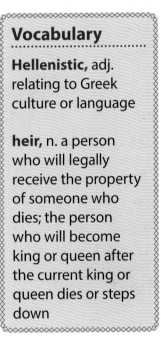

Vocabulary

Hellenistic, adj. relating to Greek culture or language

heir, n. a person who will legally receive the property of someone who dies; the person who will become king or queen after the current king or queen dies or steps down

When Alexander died so unexpectedly, he left neither an **heir** nor directions as to how his empire was to be governed. On his deathbed, he was asked to name his successor. But the weakened Alexander only muttered that the kingdom should be given "to the strongest." He didn't, or couldn't, specify who this might be.

The empire was eventually divided among five of his Greek generals. These generals fought among themselves to determine who was "the strongest." This led to much confusion and disorder, but the generals also spread Greek culture wherever they went.

Alexander had believed in the Greek system of education and wanted it established throughout his empire. He had planned to build new cities and improve old ones. He wanted the people throughout his empire to have new public buildings, theaters, and gymnasiums, like those in Athens and other Greek cities. His generals agreed with and carried out as many of his plans as they were able to. Soon, Greek soldiers, philosophers, artists, and poets were in demand throughout the Mediterranean world.

During the Hellenistic Period, kings made coins that looked like Greek coins. Educators imitated the Greek style of education. Philosophers pored over the works of Plato and Aristotle. Artists copied Greek statues, and architects built buildings in the Doric, Ionic, and Corinthian styles. In cities throughout the Middle East and Asia Minor, learning and science flourished.

Alexandria

One of the major cities of the Hellenistic Period was Alexandria, Egypt. Although it was in Egypt, Alexandria was a model Greek town. Its government was run by Greeks in the Greek style. The city was planned and built like a Greek city, including gymnasiums where male citizens could exercise and carry on conversations. Alexandria also contained important schools where philosophers could work and deepen their knowledge. It was an important center of learning and Greek culture for nearly a thousand years.

When King Ptolemy (/tahl*uh*mee/) ruled Alexandria, he began a library there that would be envied by people throughout the Mediterranean world.

The magnificent Alexandria library was in Egypt. The library contained thousands of scrolls.

It is said that he collected two hundred thousand scrolls. (Because there were no machines to print books, people wrote on sheets of papyrus, a kind of paper, and rolled the sheets up into scrolls.) When Ptolemy's son became the ruler of Alexandria, he continued to collect works of knowledge. By the 90s BCE, the main library at Alexandria had more than seven hundred thousand scrolls and was still growing. There was no other library like it in the ancient world.

For centuries, the library at Alexandria was a center of learning. Some very important thinkers of the ancient world used the library for their research. The astronomer Ptolemy worked there. His theory of how the planets, the sun, and the stars all revolve around Earth was accepted throughout Western civilization until the 1500s. Unfortunately, the library of Alexandria no longer exists. It was destroyed by a series of robberies, fires, and foreign invasions.

The Hellenistic Period was a great flowering of Greek culture. But even as Hellenistic culture flourished throughout the Mediterranean, another great civilization was growing on the Italian peninsula.

Chapter 11
The Roman Republic

The Beginnings of Rome Legend says that the city of Rome was founded by twin brothers, Romulus and Remus. According to the story, when the twins were babies, they were thrown into the Tiber River by their wicked uncle. A female wolf saved them from drowning and raised them. Once they grew up, they founded a city and named it Rome.

The Big Question

Why was the success of Rome and its lands dependent on the success of the Roman army?

Rome began as a modest settlement but became a center of power.

The story of Romulus and Remus is a myth. The actual history behind the founding of Rome is a bit harder to pin down. We know that during the 400s BCE, when Athens was experiencing its Golden Age, Rome consisted of a few thousand farmers living on some hills by the Tiber River in Italy. Eventually, several of these villages united to form one town. In time, this town, known as Rome, would become a city and the center of a great empire.

Early Rome was ruled by kings. Very little is known about this period. According to legend, six of the kings were good, kind, and just rulers, but the seventh was harsh and cruel. His name was Lucius Tarquinius Superbus (/loo*shuhs/ tahr*kwin*ee*us/ suh*purb*us/), and in about 509 BCE, the citizens of Rome rose in revolt and removed him from power.

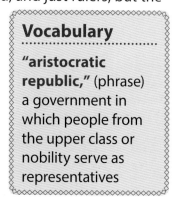

The Romans replaced their monarchy with an **aristocratic republic**. The king was replaced by two elected officials called *consuls*. These consuls

In ancient Rome, many public buildings bore the initials *SPQR*. These stood for **S**(enatus) **P**(opulusque) **R**(omanus)—The Senate and the People of Rome. This image shows the Arch of Titus, built in Rome in the 80s CE. You can see the inscription at the top of the arch.

were elected by an assembly of three hundred Roman aristocrats. The Senate, or lawmaking body, may have existed under the kings, but in the new republic, it grew more powerful. It not only elected the two new consuls every year but also advised them once they were elected.

The idea behind the republican system was that Rome should be ruled neither by a king, as it had been in its earlier days, nor by a full-fledged democracy in which every citizen could vote on every issue, as was the case in Athens. Instead, republican Rome was ruled by men chosen from among the Roman elite, including consuls and senators.

During this early period, Romans were divided into two unequal groups: **patricians** and **plebeians**. Patricians were members of the aristocracy. These noblemen held almost all the power. The best education was reserved for them, and only patricians could be members of the Senate. Plebeians were the common people. Initially, they had few rights and almost no say in how they were governed. For many years, there was even a law that prevented plebeians from marrying patricians.

For the first two centuries of Rome's existence, the patricians and plebeians were locked in a struggle with each other. The plebeians wanted rights, and the patricians wanted to keep their power. The struggle between them eventually resulted in many changes that helped to make Rome great.

> ## Vocabulary
>
> **patrician,** n. a member of ancient Rome's highest social class; a wealthy landowner in ancient Rome
>
> **plebeian,** n. a common person without power in ancient Rome
>
> **tribune,** n. in ancient Rome, an elected plebeian representative

To obtain rights and to secure themselves from injustice, the plebeians got organized. When they disagreed with the patricians' attempts to control them, they left the city and refused to listen to the patricians. The plebeians even elected their own leaders, called **tribunes**. Gradually, the plebeians forced the patricians to treat them better and to give them a voice in government.

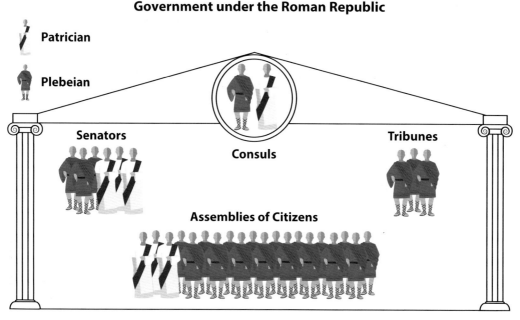

Government under the Roman Republic

Patrician

Plebeian

Senators

Consuls

Tribunes

Assemblies of Citizens

A democratic form of government developed in Rome, with both patricians and plebeians making laws for all citizens.

Eventually, the class distinctions between patricians and plebeians faded away. But there were other distinctions that never faded away. Slavery was widespread in Rome, as it had been in ancient Greece, and women had almost as few rights in Rome as they had in ancient Athens.

The Roman Republic Grows

During its early years, the city of Rome was surrounded by enemies. At first, the Romans had to defend themselves against outsiders who wanted to conquer their city. Over time, however, they began to push their enemies back. Then, the Romans began to conquer other lands and other peoples. Eventually, they would build a great empire this way.

The Roman army conquered central Italy, then northern Italy. By 275 BCE, the city of Rome governed all of Italy. Within another hundred years, they had conquered nearly all the land surrounding the Mediterranean Sea. From early on, then, Roman society was based on the army. This determined the most important ideals Romans had. Most of all, Romans admired valor, or bravery, because this was the characteristic that a good soldier needed to have.

Rome, c. 275 BCE

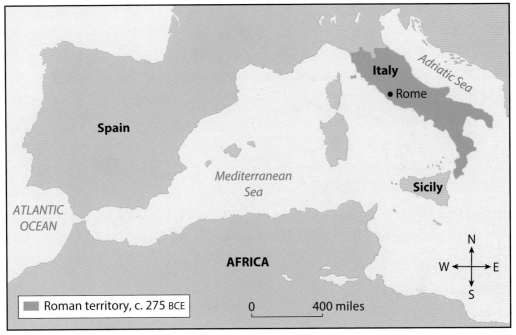

Romans admired other qualities as well, such as loyalty, duty, honor, and fidelity (faithfulness). These qualities would help them build their republic into a mighty empire.

How Romans Governed

In the beginning, the Roman army was made up of poor farmers who were forced to fight. But once the army began to conquer other peoples, soldiers could bring home things of value that they took from those they conquered. Soldiers were also given land as a reward for their service. So some began to see the benefits they could get from fighting in the army. Others saw it as an honor to belong to the Roman army.

Conquered territories were organized into **provinces**, each of which was overseen by a **governor** answerable to Rome. The Romans also stationed troops in each province to keep

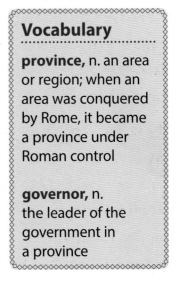

Vocabulary

province, n. an area or region; when an area was conquered by Rome, it became a province under Roman control

governor, n. the leader of the government in a province

order and to carry out decisions made by the government in Rome.

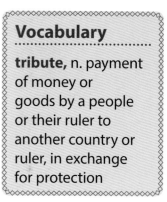
When most ancient empires conquered another people, they either wiped out the defeated people or demanded that they pay **tribute**. The Romans governed a little differently. From the beginning, they made the people they conquered part of their republic. They demanded that the people they conquered serve in their army. Like all the other soldiers in the army, if these people fought well, they were rewarded. This was different from what had happened before. Conquered people were not crushed under the heel of an occupying army; they could actually benefit from the new government.

The Romans did something else that was new. Frequently, they made these conquered people citizens of Rome. Thus, the conquered people gained political rights. They found themselves part of a growing republic that often gave them a better style of life than they had enjoyed before they were conquered.

The Romans did not do these things out of kindness. They had a purpose. It would have been impossible for a tiny group of Romans to try to control the many different peoples that were part of their growing republic. By making it in people's best interest to be loyal to the Roman Republic, and by making the city of Rome the center of everything—government, trade, and culture—the Romans were building a strong, united society.

The Republic Faces the Future

As the republic grew, so did the power of the Senate. It evolved to include wealthy plebeians as well as patricians, and it became the chief governing body of the republic. The Senate had to make decisions about all sorts of things. It passed laws, decided what the army should do, and dealt with issues at home and in the provinces. It was also a court of law and sat in judgment in certain cases.

Because the army was so successful, Rome eventually became very rich. Great amounts of stolen riches were being brought back from successful military campaigns, so Roman citizens didn't have to pay taxes. Generals and other army leaders became wealthy and spent their riches building temples and arches to celebrate their victories.

Roman men were eager to make their way in the world by being successful soldiers. They would gain wealth if they were victorious in battle, but they would also gain power. They would have important positions in society.

All of this meant that the Roman economy, system of government, and society in general relied on the continued success of the army. If Rome was to stay strong and grow, there always had to be more lands to conquer, more riches to bring home, and more citizens to include in the republic. The leading members of Roman society knew that this was important.

This way of doing things created problems, as the Romans soon learned. If the army was the place an ambitious Roman could make himself a good career, then the army was the way to power. And this way to power posed a threat to those already in power. The army could potentially be used against the Senate and the rest of the government. This was a major problem that the Romans found themselves struggling with after 100 BCE.

The Roman army was organized and powerful.

Chapter 12
The Punic Wars

The Carthaginians During the time of the early Roman Republic, the western part of the Mediterranean Sea was under the control of the wealthy city-state of Carthage. Carthage was located on the coast of North Africa, in what is now Tunisia.

The Big Question
....
What were the Punic Wars, and what was the end result?

The people of Carthage, or Carthaginians, were originally **Phoenicians** (/fih*neesh*unz/) who had come to North Africa from the Middle East about 800 BCE. The Carthaginians wanted to expand their control to Sicily, the large island off the coast of Italy that the Athenians had tried to conquer during the Peloponnesian War. Like the Athenians, the Carthaginians were having problems succeeding with their plans.

Vocabulary
....

Phoenicians, n. an ancient Mediterranean trading civilization

Punic, adj. Carthaginian; the Roman word *punicus* is Latin for Phoenician, and the Carthaginians were descendants of the Phoenicians

About 265 BCE, the Sicilians asked Rome to help keep the Carthaginians out of Sicily. The Romans were glad to help, in part because they wanted to take over Sicily for themselves. Rome's involvement in this matter, however, turned out to be much more than a one-time effort. It turned out to be the start of a series of wars known as the **Punic** (/pyoo*nihk/) Wars. These wars lasted for more than a century. At stake was control

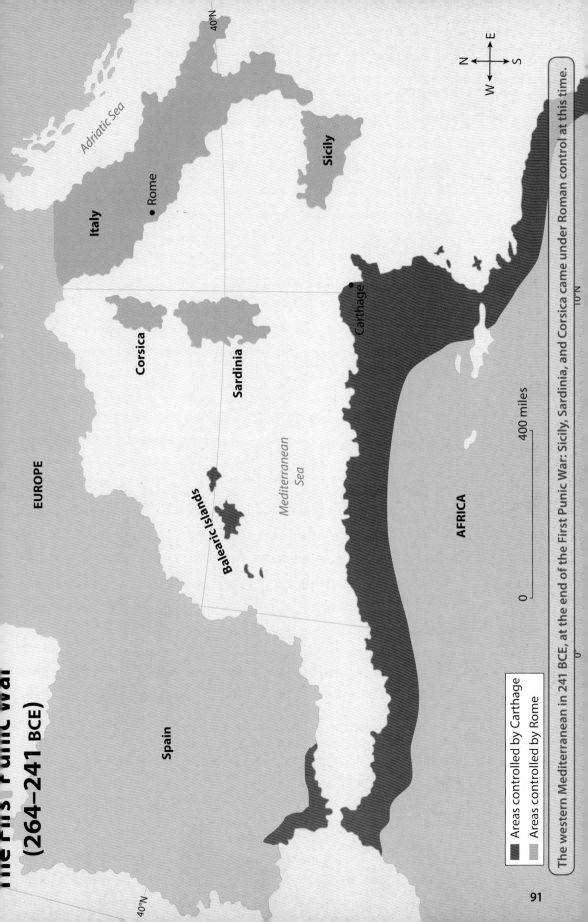

The First Punic War (264–241 BCE)

EUROPE

Spain

Balearic Islands

Corsica

Sardinia

Italy

• Rome

Adriatic Sea

40°N

Sicily

Mediterranean Sea

• Carthage

AFRICA

N
W — E
S

0   400 miles

Areas controlled by Carthage

Areas controlled by Rome

The western Mediterranean in 241 BCE, at the end of the First Punic War: Sicily, Sardinia, and Corsica came under Roman control at this time.

of the lands of the western Mediterranean, such as North Africa and Spain. Interestingly, the word *Punic* comes from the Latin word for Phoenician.

The First Punic War lasted from 264 BCE to 241 BCE. The Romans won. Rome stopped Carthage from expanding its power and control eastward. Rome also took over Sicily and made it part of the Roman Republic.

Hannibal and Scipio

Rome may have stopped Carthage from expanding eastward, but it did not stop Carthage from expanding in the west. Hamilcar Barca (/huh*mihl*kahr/ bahr*kuh/) was the general who had led Carthage's troops during the First Punic War. He managed to expand Carthage's lands in the west by taking over Spain.

Hamilcar's son, Hannibal, born in 247 BCE, had grown up hating the Romans and craving revenge for the First Punic War. In fact, he wanted nothing less than to conquer Rome completely. When Hannibal became a general at the age of twenty-six, he began to make his plans.

The treaty that ended the First Punic War set the boundaries of Carthage's empire. In 219 BCE, Hannibal decided to conquer a city near the border in Spain.

Hamilcar told his young son Hannibal stories about the First Punic War.

Second Punic War (218–201 BCE)

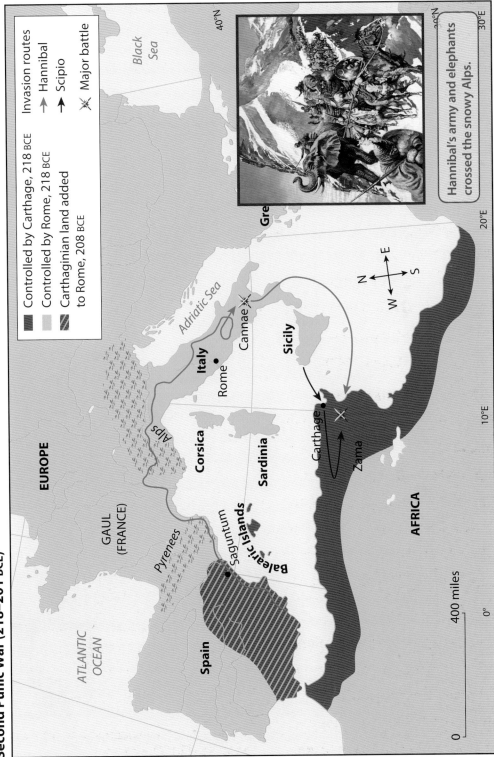

EUROPE

*ATLANTIC
OCEAN*

GAUL
(FRANCE)

Pyrenees

Spain

Saguntum

Balearic Islands

Corsica

Sardinia

Alps

Italy

Rome

Cannae ✕

Sicily

Adriatic Sea

Gre

Zama

Carthage ✕

AFRICA

*Black
Sea*

N
W · E
S

400 miles

0

40°N

30°N

0° 10°E 20°E 30°E

Invasion routes
→ Hannibal
→ Scipio
✕ Major battle

Controlled by Carthage, 218 BCE
Controlled by Rome, 218 BCE
Carthaginian land added
to Rome, 208 BCE

Hannibal's army and elephants
crossed the snowy Alps.

93

He knew that the city, Saguntum, was so close to the border that the Roman army would try to protect it. As expected, the Romans objected to Hannibal's attack on Saguntum. The battle at Saguntum started the Second Punic War, which lasted from 218 to 201 BCE.

Hannibal responded by attacking Rome. Instead of sailing across the Mediterranean Sea to Italy, Hannibal decided to attack by land. This meant leading his army through Spain, southern France, across the Alps, and into Italy. No one had ever tried this before.

Along the way, Hannibal and his army were attacked again and again by the people through whose territory they marched. Hannibal's army also included war elephants, and these had to be marched through the snowy mountain passes of the Alps. Somehow, Hannibal did it. He got his army and a handful of elephants across the Alps and into Italy.

Hannibal's men suffered a great deal on their journey, and his army was much smaller and weaker than the Roman army. But Hannibal hoped that if he could win some victories, areas of Italy would join him and revolt against Rome. Then he would be strong enough to conquer the city. By 217 BCE, Hannibal was a great general and a real threat to Rome. His army won several important battles against the Romans, but the Italians did not rise up against Rome as he had hoped. Rome refused to surrender.

Meanwhile, the Roman army attacked Carthage's armies in Spain. The war went on for years. Finally, in 206 BCE, the Romans drove the Carthaginians out of Spain completely. Then, a Roman general named Scipio Africanus (/skip*ee*oh/af*rih*kahn*us/) turned his attention to North Africa. He wanted to conquer the city of Carthage itself.

Hannibal had been unable to advance farther in Italy and had even begun to lose ground. When Scipio attacked North Africa, Hannibal decided to help defend the city of Carthage. He and his army abandoned Italy and returned home to do whatever they could.

The city of Carthage was forced to surrender in the Second Punic War.

In the battle of Zama, southwest of Carthage, in 202 BCE, Hannibal lost twenty thousand men, and Scipio was victorious. Carthage gave up and was forced to pay Rome for its losses in the war.

Although the war was over, Hannibal refused to give up. He would not turn himself over to the Romans. For several years, the Romans kept demanding that Hannibal surrender. The Roman army chased him from place to place, trying to capture him. Finally, about the year 183 BCE, they managed to corner him. Unable to escape, Hannibal still would not turn himself over to his hated enemy. He poisoned himself and died.

The Third Punic War

Carthage lost the Second Punic War. But the city had caused so much trouble for so long that the Romans still considered Carthage their worst enemy. Carthage had little political power left, but it still had a good deal of influence on trade in the Mediterranean. Even though the Roman Republic was still growing and prospering, there were Romans who wanted to see Carthage destroyed once and for all. One person who felt this way was the Roman senator known as Cato the Elder. Cato (/kayt*oh/) ended every speech he made in the Roman Senate with the words "Carthage must be destroyed." Romans who shared his point of view waited and watched for the right opportunity.

In 150 BCE, Carthage defended itself against an attack by a small army. This broke the treaty that had ended the Second Punic War. Carthage had used military force again, and Rome used this as an excuse to send its army against Carthage.

The leaders of Carthage did not want to fight the Romans. They asked for peace and agreed to surrender their weapons. But the Romans told them they would have to leave the city and go far inland, away from the Mediterranean **trade routes** that were so important to them. This was too much for the citizens of Carthage. Trade was their livelihood.

> **Vocabulary**
>
> **trade route,** n. a road or waterway traveled by merchants or traders to buy or sell goods

Carthage refused to listen to the Romans any longer. In 147 BCE, Scipio Aemilianus (/ee*mih*lee*ay*nus/) attacked Carthage. He was the adopted grandson of the famous Roman general Scipio Africanus, who had fought in the Second Punic War. The battle for Carthage was long and bitter.

In the end, the Roman army conquered the city. Out of a population of 250,000, only fifty thousand remained alive at the end of the battle.

The End of the Third Punic War (146 BCE)

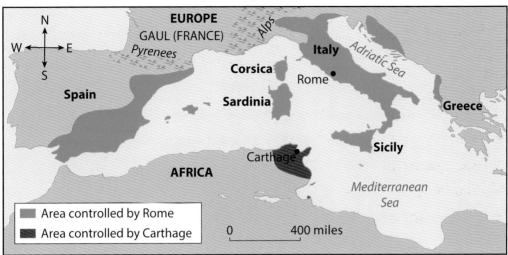

The survivors were sold into slavery, and the Roman army leveled the city. It had taken three wars and a hundred years to break the power of Carthage, but by the end of the Third Punic War it was finally broken.

Romans and Greeks

With Carthage destroyed, Rome became the dominant power in the Mediterranean. The Romans soon conquered the Hellenistic kingdoms that had been established after the death of Alexander the Great, including Greece itself. But in another sense, the Greeks also conquered the Romans, for the Romans were won over by Greek culture.

Greek literature, art, and architecture became a mighty influence on Roman culture. Wealthy Romans had Greek sculptures brought to Italy, where they ordered copies and imitations made. Roman authors began imitating Greek authors, and Roman students began studying Greek literature and philosophy. Thus, the victory over Carthage led not only to the Romanizing of the Greeks but also to the Hellenizing of the Romans.

Chapter 13
Julius Caesar: A Great Roman

Hail to the Conqueror! In the years after the Punic Wars, Rome continued to look for new areas to conquer and new peoples to govern. The young men of Rome's most powerful families were eager to gain fame by leading a Roman army in battle.

The Big Question

How would you describe the character of Julius Caesar, and what brought about his fall from power?

They looked forward to the wealth, honor, and power they would gain if they succeeded. Julius Caesar, who lived from 101–44 BCE, was one of these ambitious young men.

Caesar belonged to a patrician family, but he was not wealthy. He knew that if he was going to get ahead in life, he would have to do it through military advancement. Caesar lived at a time when the Roman Republic was beginning to have problems. The consuls and the Senate still ruled, but governors in the provinces were not always just and often forced people to pay high taxes. People in some of the conquered territories were unhappy about how they were governed. Rome had to rely on the strength of the army to keep the republic together.

The Roman army had changed, too. It was no longer manned by ordinary citizens. It had become a professional army. This meant that the men who joined

Julius Caesar

the army did so to further their careers. They were willing to fight, but mostly they wanted to get rich and gain higher status. They felt more loyalty to the generals who could lead them to victory, and who would give them the rewards of war, than they did to Rome itself.

The army had always been important to the Roman Republic, but now it was more important than ever. The generals who led the army were extremely powerful and could do great good or great harm. It was just a matter of time before someone tried to take over the republic completely. Julius Caesar was that someone.

The Rise to Power

Caesar was tall and well-built. He had dark-brown eyes and cared about how he looked. He kept his hair trimmed and his face clean-shaven. Caesar was intelligent and had a good sense of humor. He could be charming and courteous when he wanted to be. But because Caesar was a very ambitious and determined man he could also be ruthless.

Caesar commanded part of the Roman army, but that was not enough for him. He wanted as much power as he could get. Caesar knew that to get what he wanted, he would have to be victorious in battle. Then, his soldiers would be more loyal to him than to Rome. He would also need political allies in Rome. If he helped others get some of the power they wanted, he could use them to get the power that he wanted.

To become powerful at this time, it was important to be popular with the right people in Rome. So Caesar spent money entertaining others and making friends. Once he was popular, Caesar entered into an alliance with two other powerful Roman men named Pompey (/pahm*pee/) and Crassus (/kras*us/). They helped one another to pass laws they wanted and schemed to hold onto the power that their enemies wanted to take from them. Caesar became powerful enough to be elected consul in 59 BCE.

Caesar led the campaign against Gaul, which today we know as France.

Julius Caesar became one of the most successful generals the Roman army had ever seen. He helped expand the Roman Republic in Europe. It took him about nine years to fight the **Gallic Wars**, which gave Rome power in Gaul (present-day France). He even invaded Britain in 55 BCE, although Rome would not conquer the island until the next century. Much of northern Europe was coming under the control of the Mediterranean world and would be influenced by the culture and laws of the Romans.

Vocabulary

Gallic Wars, n. wars between Rome and the people of Gaul, which today is the country of France

After he had conquered Gaul, Caesar decided that he wanted to be elected consul again—his previous consulship had ended. The first time he had been consul, however, he had been proud and arrogant. He did some things he should not have done. Worse, his alliance with Pompey and Crassus had broken down. Pompey, in particular, did not trust Caesar anymore and wanted to remove him from power.

No one becomes powerful without making enemies, and he had made some powerful ones. Now these enemies were determined to keep him from becoming consul again. They told Caesar that if he wanted to be elected consul, he had to come to Rome for the election. They also reminded him that he was not allowed to bring his army into Rome. But Caesar knew that if he went to Rome without his army, Pompey would have him arrested. Caesar faced a difficult choice. He wanted to be consul again, but it seemed impossible without breaking the law and taking at least part of his army into the city.

Dictator for Life

Caesar was not afraid to do things the hard way. In 49 BCE, he gathered his army and marched toward Rome. By crossing the Rubicon River, the northern boundary of Italy, he showed the Senate that he would fight them for power. Caesar understood that there was no turning back. Legend has it that when he crossed the Rubicon he said, "The die is cast." Today, we use the phrase "the die is cast" to mean taking decisive action. Similarly, the phrase "crossing the Rubicon" has come to mean going past the point of no return.

Caesar's actions started a **civil war**. Caesar and his army now had to fight with other parts of the Roman army. The existence of the Roman Republic itself was at stake.

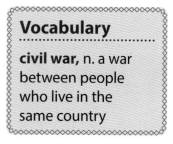

Vocabulary

civil war, n. a war between people who live in the same country

Caesar quickly took control of Italy, but Pompey and his army managed to escape. Caesar chased them down until the two armies clashed in Greece. Pompey was defeated in Pharsalus, Greece, and fled to Egypt, where he was killed. Caesar made his way to Egypt and continued fighting Pompeian forces loyal to the old republic in North Africa and Spain. At last, in 44 BCE, Caesar achieved what he had wanted all along. He became the dictator, or absolute ruler, of Rome.

Caesar led his army across the Rubicon toward Rome, showing that he was willing to fight to stay in power.

The Romans had known dictators before. In fact, they felt that in times of emergency, a dictator was necessary. But dictatorship was seen as a temporary thing, to be used only in wartime. Legally, dictatorships could only last six months.

This Roman coin shows Julius Caesar wearing a wreath.

Caesar had something else in mind. He thought the idea of a temporary dictator was foolish. Who would willingly give up ultimate power simply because the Senate told him to? Caesar was not going to give up the power he had gained. He made sure that everyone knew he meant to be the ruler for a long time. He had his face put on coins, (something only kings did at this time), and the month of Quintilis was renamed Julius (July) in his honor.

Caesar had always loved the attention that he got from being a public figure. Nothing pleased him more than the privilege of wearing a laurel wreath, the symbol of conquerors and victors. But opponents said it looked like he was wearing a royal crown.

During the five years after Caesar had crossed the Rubicon, he gained absolute power. True, he spent a lot of his time making sure that his enemies could not overthrow him, but he also genuinely tried to improve things for people. Caesar had plans to make more people Roman citizens, stop corruption, improve the court system, and help people avoid falling into debt. He seemed to work constantly. He dictated letters while he was riding to battle. He worked quickly and tirelessly, but there was simply more work than one man could do.

Out of Touch

Caesar found it difficult to give other people things to do. In part, this was because he distrusted everyone and wanted to be in complete control.

But it was also true that many government officials wouldn't cooperate with him because they were horrified by the bloody civil wars that pitted Roman against Roman. Many blamed Caesar for the collapse of the republic.

The pressures of being dictator began to make Caesar sick. He became exhausted, tense, and irritable. His health was affected. He felt dizzy and suffered from convulsions and blackouts. In addition, accounts from the time said he suffered from epilepsy. Epilepsy is a medical condition that affects the nervous system and causes sudden convulsions and blackouts.

Although Caesar had been an excellent general, he was not an especially good dictator. He was arrogant and offended many powerful Romans. He even dismissed his bodyguards, saying that no one could possibly want to murder him because his death would only bring about chaos.

Although Julius Caesar had the Senate make him dictator for life, he had made a great many enemies.

This showed that Caesar was seriously out of touch. He did not recognize how much some people hated him. Then, in February of 44 BCE, Caesar went even further. He had the Senate vote him dictator for life.

There had long been powerful people in Rome who did not like the fact that Caesar had become dictator. Once he became dictator for life, even more people grew angry. To many, having a dictator for life was no different than having a king. They blamed Caesar for destroying the republic, and now they were prepared to do something about it.

The Betrayal

Caesar never seemed to realize how much pain he had caused the Roman people when he forced Roman to fight against Roman in the civil wars he started. He never seemed to realize that Romans were proud of the republic and did not want to see the days of the kings brought back. This shortsightedness contributed to his downfall.

About a month after he was made dictator for life, Caesar was murdered in the Senate house by several members of the Roman Senate. There were about sixty **conspirators**, although only a handful actually drove their weapons into Caesar. The leaders of the **assassination** plot were Brutus (/broot*us/) and Cassius. Tradition has it that as he was being stabbed, Caesar noticed Brutus among the men surrounding him and said, "Et tu, Brute?" (/et/tu/broo*tay/) This is Latin for "You too, Brutus?" He had considered Brutus a friend and was shocked that Brutus had conspired against him.

> **Vocabulary**
>
> **conspirator,** n. a person who plans or participates with others in a crime
>
> **assassination,** n. the murder of a public figure, such as a government official

Julius Caesar was assassinated in the Senate house.

Caesar had destroyed the republic in his quest for power, but he had not had the time—or perhaps the ability—to put a new form of government in its place. His assassination ended his rule and left the leaders of Rome to try to figure out who should rule in his place.

Julius Caesar is remembered today as a great general who did much to increase the power of Rome. Although he destroyed the Roman Republic, he also paved the way for the Roman Empire. He is the link between the republic that Rome had been and the empire it would become.

Chapter 14
The Age of Augustus

New Beginning Julius Caesar's assassination led to another civil war. After thirteen years of fighting, Octavian, the great nephew of Julius Caesar, became sole ruler of Rome and all its provinces.

The Big Question

Why might Augustus have wanted to glorify Rome?

This was no easy task. Octavian had to defeat Brutus and Cassius, the conspirators who had killed Caesar. He also had to defeat Mark Antony, who was romantically and militarily allied with Cleopatra, the queen of Egypt. By 27 BCE, however, Octavian had defeated all of these rivals and established himself as the first Roman emperor. To celebrate this achievement, the Roman Senate named him Caesar Augustus.

Although Augustus was related to Julius Caesar, the two men were very different. Unlike his great uncle, Augustus was not interested in what he wore or how he looked. From the time he was young, he had suffered from bad health. Although he was a busy man, it seems he hated getting up early. He would sleep as late and as long as possible.

Caesar Augustus became the first Roman emperor.

Augustus was also different from Julius Caesar in another important way. Julius Caesar had been a brave soldier but a bad **administrator**. Augustus avoided battle as much as possible and was never known as a good soldier, but he turned out to be a very good administrator.

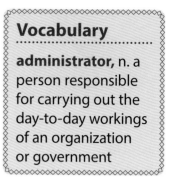
Augustus realized that Romans had stopped feeling proud of themselves and their empire. They had experienced years of warfare, and it must have seemed like the government didn't care about them. Augustus knew that for the Roman Empire to be strong, Romans had to believe in it. So he made some changes.

The Altar of Peace (*Ara Pacis*) was built to celebrate the return of Augustus to Rome in 13 BCE, after a military campaign in Spain and in Gaul (France).

To restore Romans' confidence, Augustus began an ambitious building program. He brought architects, sculptors, and artists to Rome to create beautiful buildings. He had his architects copy the majesty of Greek architecture and art. His buildings were often made of marble, and he spared no expense. He built great arches celebrating events in Roman history and had statues of great Romans made. All of this helped promote the image of Rome as the capital of an empire that stood for order, strength, honor, and permanence. Romans could be proud. Later, Augustus would boast, "I found Rome as bricks. I leave it to you as marble."

Augustus rebuilt the temples and reestablished the religion of the Romans so that people could believe in the old gods and goddesses again. By making religion part of being a good citizen, Augustus was giving Romans a sense of identity. He helped them figure out who they were and what they believed. He gave them the feeling that they were part of something great. After years of chaos, Rome had a new beginning.

Virgil

As part of his program to make Romans proud again, Augustus encouraged the arts. Like wealthy rulers before and after him (including Pericles), he became a patron of the arts.

Maecenas (/my*see*nus/), one of the friends of Augustus and a rich and important politician, was also someone who supported the arts. For years, he invited poets to write about Augustus and all he was doing for the empire. One of the poets he talked to was a man named Publius Vergilius Maro, known as Virgil.

Like the other Roman poets at this time, Virgil admired Greek poetry and imitated its style. He wanted to write a great poem that would celebrate the glory of Rome, but he disagreed with Maecenas's suggestion that the poem should be mainly about Augustus. Virgil had a different idea.

Virgil wrote the epic poem, the *Aeneid*.

The *Aeneid*

The poem that Virgil wrote for Augustus and Maecenas is called the *Aeneid* (/ee*nee*ihd/). It is the greatest epic poem produced in ancient Rome. The *Aeneid* tells the story of Aeneas (/ee*nee*us/), a great warrior who survived the defeat of the **Trojans** during the Trojan War and who journeyed across the Mediterranean to found Rome. All along the way, Aeneas ran into obstacles and temptations. For instance, a beautiful queen of Carthage named Dido fell in

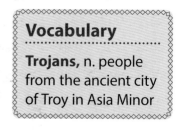

Vocabulary

Trojans, n. people from the ancient city of Troy in Asia Minor love with him and tried to get him to stay with her. But Aeneas knew that it was his destiny to establish a great city in Italy, so he left Dido heartbroken and continued on. Aeneas refused to allow anything to stand between him and his destiny.

Virgil died before he completed the *Aeneid,* but his epic poem remains a great piece of literature and a powerful piece of Roman **propaganda**. The *Aeneid* gave the Romans an exciting past and a national hero, and it taught them that Rome was worth the sacrifices that Aeneas had made.

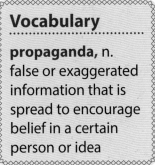

Vocabulary

propaganda, n. false or exaggerated information that is spread to encourage belief in a certain person or idea

Augustus was excited about Virgil's poem and begged to see parts of it as the poet worked on it. Even though it wasn't a poem about him, Augustus knew that the *Aeneid* was exactly the kind of literature he wanted. He knew that this poem glorified Rome and would make the citizens love the Roman Empire.

Law and Order

Unlike Julius Caesar, who had shortsightedly forgotten that many Romans would hate a king or any other absolute ruler, Augustus always remembered how easy it would be to assassinate him. So he took care to include the Senate in the responsibilities of ruling. He never gave up power and never believed in democracy, but he was careful about how he ruled. Augustus avoided Julius Caesar's mistake of being arrogant. He modestly called himself the *princeps* (/prihn*keps/), or first citizen. The Senate gave him another title—that of *Imperator*, or emperor, meaning he who commands.

During his reign as emperor, Augustus accomplished several things. Among the greatest of these was the strengthening of Roman law. Augustus made it clear that, while he was a powerful ruler, the law limited his power. The Senate and other Roman leaders knew that he had some responsibilities and they had other responsibilities. This helped to establish confidence in the emperor and in Roman rule.

Augustus also changed the way the military was run. He divided the army into two parts. The first part was made up of twenty-seven **legions** of Roman citizens. This amounted to about 165,000 troops in total. Each legion was commanded by a senator who had to report to more powerful senators, who in turn reported to Augustus. This system was meant to ensure that no individual senator would control an army strong enough to attack Rome.

Each Roman legion contained thousands of men.

The second part of the army was made up of men who were not Roman citizens. They were commanded by noblemen and divided into sections that were smaller than the legions. These men could gain citizenship after they served in the army. So even those who were not from wealthy or powerful families could serve in this part of the army and make good careers for themselves.

In the past, the Roman army had been supported by the riches it gathered after victories. Augustus changed this as well. Generals and soldiers could still get rich from the **spoils** they took, but the army would be supported and supplied by Rome. Augustus established a special **treasury** just for the army. This meant that generals had to depend on Rome for supplies. They would be less likely to want to turn on Rome because if they did, the Senate would cut off their supplies. By making these changes, Augustus was trying to ensure that there would never be another Julius Caesar to threaten Rome—or any other rivals to threaten Augustus himself.

Vocabulary

spoils, n. property or valuables taken by the winner in a conflict

treasury, n. a place where the money and other riches of a government are kept

Pax Romana, n. literally, Roman peace; a period of about two hundred years without major conflicts in the Roman Empire

By this time, the empire had become about as large as it could be. Despite good Roman roads, it could take more than a year to cross it. So now the army was mainly used to keep order.

Law and order brought peace to the Roman Empire. Called the **Pax Romana**, or Roman peace, this was a time of calm and law throughout the Mediterranean world. It would last nearly two hundred years.

Such a long time of peace had never been experienced within an empire before. Centuries later, people from many different parts of the world would admire the Pax Romana and try to achieve something similar in their own countries.

The Roman Empire

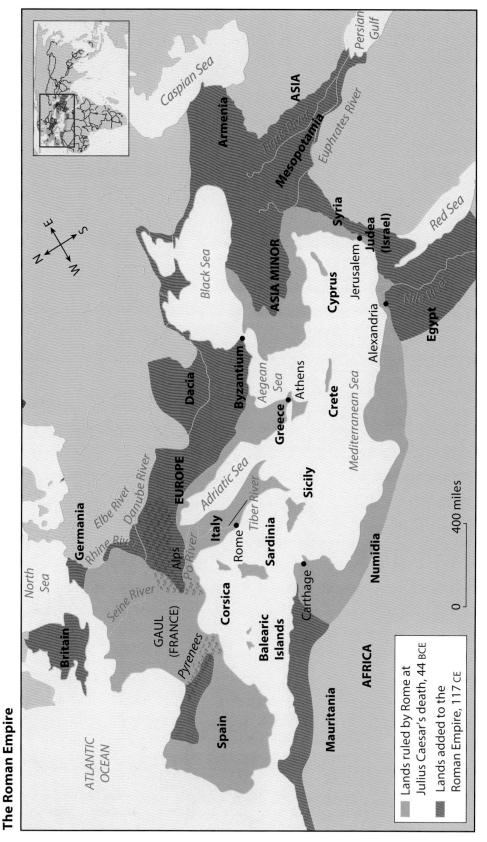

At its height, the Roman Empire stretched over two million square miles.

Caesar Augustus was the first emperor of the Roman Empire. He established the empire and ruled it well. He understood how to work with the Senate, how to help citizens feel proud of Rome, and how to use the army to keep a peace that lasted for centuries. For all of these reasons, Augustus is remembered as one of Rome's greatest leaders.

Chapter 15
Rome and Christianity

New Religion The Roman Empire must
have been an interesting place to live. Its
population came from a wide range of
backgrounds and spoke many different
languages. They practiced different
religions and believed in all kinds of gods
and goddesses. In addition, between
27 BCE and 180 CE, the Pax Romana made it possible for people
to travel around the empire peacefully and easily.

The Big Question

Why was the growth
of Christianity
originally considered
a threat to the
Roman Empire?

People of all kinds moved across the Roman Empire. Some traded or visited Roman cities; others moved to these cities to work in them.

In the marketplace of one of the cities in the empire, such as Antioch or Damascus, one might find goods from faraway places, see Roman soldiers, and meet people from all over. Not only traders and merchants could be found in the marketplace but also teachers and philosophers,

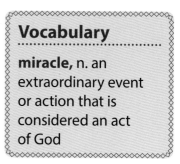
would-be healers and **miracle** workers, and preachers of new religions.

About the year 40 CE, people in the larger cities of the empire began to hear stories about a new religion in which the followers believed in a man called Jesus Christ. They heard that he had been a Jew from Palestine. His followers said he had died and been raised to life again. He was going to come back to Earth and bring the Kingdom of God. His followers believed all this so strongly that many of them had changed their lives completely. A few of his followers, including a man named Paul, traveled around the empire, trying to convince people to believe in this Christ.

Most Romans ignored the new religion. In the cities of the empire, especially, there was always someone with a new religion, a new report of a miracle, or a prophecy about the future. These Christians, or followers of Christ, were just one tiny part of a large complicated empire. But others paid more attention to these Christians, and that attention was not always favorable.

Rome Feels Threatened

Jesus had lived in Palestine and had preached first to the Jewish community. His first followers continued to spread his teachings among the Jews of the Middle East. Very quickly, however, there were disagreements within the Jewish community about these new Christian ideas. Some of these disagreements caused conflict.

Gradually, Judaism and Christianity became two different religions with very different beliefs. Christians continued to preach around the empire and start new communities.

The painter Raphael depicted Saint Paul preaching in Athens, Greece.

Sometimes there were problems between Christians and people who had an interest in preserving other religions. The early Christian preacher Paul was once arrested in the city of Ephesus (/ef*ih*sus/) because silversmiths who made statues of a Greek goddess felt that he was hurting their business. In other places, Christians were beaten or arrested because their attempts at preaching started arguments in public. Christians were also blamed for other problems that developed. Because Christians were a new group that people didn't know much about, they were easy to blame.

During the 100s and 200s CE, the Roman Empire faced serious troubles. The empire had grown so large that it took a long time for communications to travel between Rome and other cities. The army and governors of provinces were often cruel or corrupt. Worse, people outside the empire, especially in Europe, began to try to conquer parts of it.

The Romans knew their empire would be strong and united if people were loyal. To the Romans, loyalty meant several things. It meant paying taxes to Rome, and it meant taking part in **rituals** and ceremonies that were part of the Roman process of government. Many of these rituals and ceremonies were religious and required making offerings to

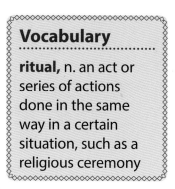
the gods, who were believed to protect Rome. The Romans had many gods and goddesses. Some emperors, such as Julius Caesar and Augustus, had even been declared gods after they died. The Romans were also clear about what happened to people who were not loyal. They held public executions to make their point. People who were not loyal risked horrible deaths.

As the numbers of Christians grew, they were often seen as troublemakers. But were they actually disloyal to Rome?

Christians claimed that they were loyal to Rome. They pointed to one of Jesus's teachings: "Render unto Caesar the things which are Caesar's; and unto God the things that are God's" (Matthew 22:21). For Christians, this was clear proof that there was no conflict between Christian faith and Roman citizenship. A Christian could pay the taxes that the emperors required and remain loyal to the Roman government while worshiping and obeying God.

But the Romans weren't so sure. They began requiring Christians to make offerings to Roman gods and goddesses to prove that they were good citizens, and to ensure that the traditional gods and goddesses continued to protect Rome. Christians refused to do this because they felt the Roman gods and goddesses were false. They only offered worship to their own God. When they refused to obey the Romans, they were arrested and sometimes executed. Some were thrown to wild beasts to be torn apart and eaten, and others were forced to participate in gladiator battles.

Colosseums were circular, stone structures that were centers for entertainment, including hand-to-hand combat. Christians were also forced to fight for their lives in colosseums, as this painting from the 1800s shows.

Gladiators were enslaved men, prisoners of war, or condemned criminals whose lives the Romans already considered worthless. These people were sometimes forced to fight to the death against wild animals or one another in Roman colosseums.

Until 310 CE, Christians faced **persecution** throughout the Roman Empire, at times just because they were Christians. Although the persecution did not take place everywhere and was not continual, this was a difficult time for the growing Christian Church.

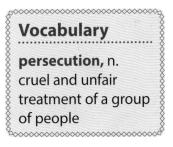

Vocabulary

persecution, n. cruel and unfair treatment of a group of people

At first, Roman leaders seemed to think that persecuting Christians would make citizens more loyal and the empire more united. Instead, the opposite happened. Many people eventually came to sympathize with those who were killed for being disloyal. The persecuted Christians were admired for their calm, courage, and willingness to stand up for their beliefs. These same characteristics were also important to the Romans.

Christians were also well organized, another characteristic that the Romans admired. They belonged to communities and had leaders. They could efficiently gather donations and resources to help when people—including non-Christians—faced disaster from fires, floods, or famines. Moreover, it meant something to be a Christian during a time when people were beginning to wonder whether being Roman meant anything. To become a Christian, a person had to go through a period of training and study. Christians were expected to live their lives according to their beliefs. Not every Christian did, of course, especially as the Church grew larger. But the expectation was there.

A Christian Roman Empire

By the beginning of the 300s CE, the Roman Empire seemed to be falling apart. Christianity was the strongest, fastest growing religion in the empire. Then something happened to change things. On the eve of a battle, the Battle of Milvian Bridge on October 2, 312 CE, Emperor Constantine had a vision in which he believed the Christian God promised him victory. In that moment, Constantine became a Christian. His **conversion** was also the glue needed to hold the empire together.

In 313 CE, Constantine signed the **Edict** of Milan. This document made Christianity a legal religion. Christians no longer had to prove their loyalty to the Roman Empire. They had the right to be part of the empire. From this point on, Christianity prospered in the Roman Empire. More and more people became Christians, and Constantine actively promoted the religion as a way to strengthen the empire. Some say that he was **baptized** on his deathbed. His mother had been a Christian, but throughout a large part of his life, he was not. Still,

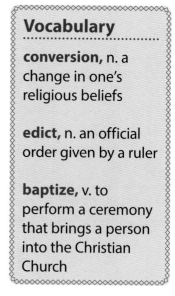

Vocabulary

conversion, n. a change in one's religious beliefs

edict, n. an official order given by a ruler

baptize, v. to perform a ceremony that brings a person into the Christian Church

because the Roman Empire eventually became a Christian empire, Constantine is remembered as a Christian emperor. Almost all his successors were devoted Christians, and by the end of the 300s, they were persecuting followers of Rome's old **pagan** religions.

The image shows an ancient Roman mosaic of Emperor Constantine.

Chapter 16
The Fall of the Roman Empire

Strengths and Weaknesses The Roman Empire accomplished a lot for the people who lived within its boundaries. The Romans brought their own brand of law and order to the lands around the Mediterranean Sea. They built roads. Originally used to move the army from one area to the next, these roads were also used for trade and travel.

The Big Question

What caused the decline and fall of the western Roman Empire?

The Romans built cities throughout their empire, and they improved the quality of food and water available in most places. Good government and laws protected the rights of Roman citizens and gave people the opportunity to seek justice for wrongs. The Roman Empire brought peace and prosperity that lasted for centuries.

By the 200s CE, however, the empire was struggling with serious problems. For a long time, Romans were prosperous because the empire was continually growing. New people, lands, and trade possibilities were always being added to the empire. The army brought back riches and added new sources of tax money. But by the 200s CE, the empire had stopped growing.

Romans built roads across their empire. Roads were needed for soldiers, but they were also needed to more easily transport goods from place to place.

Money Troubles

The empire began to show signs of weakness. Some of these were **economic**. By the year 200 CE, there was a significant **recession**. This meant that there were fewer jobs and fewer goods available. Recessions are often accompanied by periods of **inflation**, and that is what happened in the Roman Empire. During a time of inflation, money is available but not worth much, so prices rise. People have to pay more and more for the things they want to buy.

The emperors tried to address the problems that came with recession and inflation. The emperor Diocletian (/dye*uh*klee*shun/) (284–305 CE) thought that he could stop prices from rising by declaring what the prices should be. This did not improve matters. The only thing that happened was that some goods became completely unavailable.

Emperor Constantine (274–337 CE) thought that the problem with high prices was that more money was needed. He took gold from the pagan temples and turned it into money, but this did not help either. Inflation did not stop, and other problems developed. Recession and inflation combined to cause joblessness. With joblessness came poverty, and with poverty came crime and disease. Some Roman leaders tried giving away money and bread, but these were short-term fixes to problems that were large and complicated.

Vocabulary

economic, adj. relating to the management of money and resources to produce, buy, and sell goods and services

recession, n. a time of reduced economic activity, when there is little buying or selling

inflation, n. a rise in prices and a fall in the purchasing value of money

On this ancient Roman coin, you can see the emperor Constantine.

Gap Between Rich and Poor

Additionally, the gap between the rich and the poor widened. Aristocrats, such as senators, were five times richer than they had been in the Age of Augustus. And there were fewer and fewer opportunities for people to improve their future. The Roman army had been one place where many men had gained wealth, land, and social position. However, the army was no longer conquering new territories. In fact, it was struggling to hold on to lands that had been conquered many years before.

Government also suffered serious problems. Powerful generals and the army legions loyal to them battled for power. General murdered general. It seemed as if civil war had become a way of life. Officials became increasingly corrupt and did not do their jobs properly.

Some emperors were good and wise, but others were totally unsuited to ruling. For example, Nero, who reigned from 54 to 68 CE, was probably insane. He had his mother stabbed to death and his first and second wives were killed. One was executed; the other was murdered. He was accused of setting fire to the city of Rome—a crime that he blamed on Christians, whom he cruelly put to death. (Today, most historians have concluded that it is unlikely that Nero caused the fire.) At last, the army forced him to commit suicide. Before he died, Nero supposedly said, "Death! And so great an artist." Other emperors poisoned their enemies and neglected the affairs of the empire. Between 180 and 270 CE there were eighty emperors—almost one a year—and many of them were worthless.

People wondered whether there was any justice in the world. It seemed that greed and corruption were everywhere in the empire. They began to wonder whether there was anything worth believing in.

During this time, the number of Christians continued to grow. Christianity seemed to offer what many in the empire were looking for. Some were drawn to Christianity because it preached peace in a time of violence. Others were

Nero blamed the Christians for the fire that broke out in Rome in 64 CE.

drawn to Christianity because it gave opportunities for talented men to become leaders without having to kill to gain power. Talented, educated men were needed to lead the Church, and Church leaders did not lead by force and violence. During the 200s CE, Christians were still not considered loyal citizens of the empire, and they still faced persecution. After the Edict of Milan in 313 CE, however, they could be found throughout society.

The troubles of the 200s and 300s CE were so serious that it seemed like the empire would collapse. Bur the problems inside the empire were only part of the story.

The Germanic Tribes

For the Romans, the center of the world was Rome, and Rome was part of the Mediterranean world. Their attention was drawn to the lands and peoples that surrounded the Mediterranean Sea. Once Rome had conquered all of these, their generals looked for other ways to expand the empire. Men such as Julius Caesar fought wars in Europe to bring the peoples of the North under Roman control. Caesar and a few other Romans went as far as Britain and established bases there.

The peoples of northern Europe, however, were not like the familiar peoples of the Mediterranean. The Romans referred to northern Europeans as barbarians. Unlike the peoples of the Mediterranean, some of the peoples of Europe did not settle in one place. They moved from place to place in search of adequate sources of food, and at times because of conflicts with others. They did not build large cities like the ones in other parts of the Roman Empire, and they offered fewer opportunities for trade with Rome.

Goths and Vandals

One significant group of northern people included Germanic tribes, such as the Goths and the Vandals. For several centuries, these tribes bothered the Romans by attacking Roman soldiers and trying to invade the empire. Most of these attacks were small and not well organized. Such attacks were not really a threat to the empire when it was strong, but now the empire had its own problems and was not as strong as it had been. The Germanic tribes began to be successful when they attacked Roman troops.

Many of the so-called barbarians were fierce fighters. The Romans admired this. In places when they were able to, they included these warriors in the army legions that patrolled the borders of the empire. After a time, the Roman army that patrolled the northern borders of the empire was mostly made up of warriors from Germanic tribes. They fought off the attacks of other Germanic tribes. At least they were supposed to.

In 410 CE, the Visigothic king Alaric (/al*uh*rihk/) and his army invaded the empire and attacked the city of Rome. They overcame Rome's defenses and **plundered** it. The Roman leaders in the

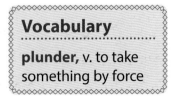

Vocabulary

plunder, v. to take something by force

eastern part of the empire were shocked that the western Roman leaders had let it come to this. The western part of the empire was in chaos. The last Roman emperor in the west was Romulus Augustulus. He was overthrown by Odoacer (/oh*doh*ay*sur/), a Germanic warrior. Odoacer became the first barbarian king of Italy. He ruled until 493 CE when he was overthrown by Theodoric (/thee*ah*duh*rihk/), king of the Ostrogoths. At this point, Roman rule no longer existed in western Europe and the western part of the Mediterranean.

In 410 CE, the Visigoths, led by King Alaric, attacked and plundered Rome.

The Rise of Islam

Roman rule still existed in the east, which had long been the wealthier and more important part of the empire. Increasingly, it was also called the Byzantine (/bihz*un*teen/) Empire. There was an emperor in the great city of Constantinople, which Emperor Constantine had founded as the "New Rome." (Constantine founded Constantinople in a place formerly known as Byzantium which is where the Byzantine Empire got its name. Today, this city is called Istanbul and is in Turkey.) The Eastern Roman (or Byzantine) Empire ruled over the lands that today are Greece and Turkey. At different times, the Eastern Roman Empire also ruled over parts of the Middle East.

In 610 CE, a man named Muhammad, who lived in Arabia, began to see visions. He was regarded as a holy **prophet** by many and soon became the leader of a new religion: Islam. Muhammad united

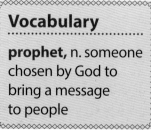

Vocabulary

prophet, n. someone chosen by God to bring a message to people

the Arabs, who had long been fighting, and gave them a sense of purpose. They became followers of Allah and students of a holy book called the Koran.

Islam grew as a religion. Within several years, the Arabs had joined together as Muslims. Anyone who was not a Muslim was classified as an unbeliever. Many Muslims felt that it was lawful to make war on unbelievers.

The Arab armies began to attack the Byzantine Empire from the south. The city of Antioch in Syria fell in 637 CE. Alexandria in Egypt fell in 642 CE. In the early 700s, Muslim armies conquered Spain. However an attempt to invade Gaul (France) was stopped by a Christian army in 732 CE.

The Eastern Roman Empire, or Byzantine Empire, with its capital in Constantinople, remained standing. It would last for almost a thousand years, although it was attacked a number of times. Finally, in 1453 CE,

This medieval painting from the 1400s shows the city of Constantinople.

Constantinople was conquered, and the emperor was killed. The Byzantine Empire, which had always considered itself an extension of the Roman Empire, had fallen at last.

The Grandeur That Was Rome

The decline and fall of Rome was a long, slow process. It had many causes, and there was no single moment, event, or decision that could have stopped it. Problems within the empire and challenges from outside combined to bring the empire in the west to an end. Yet even when there was no longer a Roman emperor in Rome, people still thought in terms of the empire.

Christian leaders took on many of the duties of Roman officials. They divided the Church along the same lines as the empire in the west had been divided. Over centuries, the Roman official called a *vicarius* became a church vicar, a minister or priest in charge of a church. A *diocese*, originally an area for Roman administration, became an area of church administration. Church leaders continued to wear the same clothing, or *vestitus,* that Roman officials had worn. Today, these items are referred to as vestments, the garments worn for religious rituals.

The prestige of the old Roman Empire was so strong that in 800 CE, a king of the Franks named Charlemagne was named "Holy Roman Emperor." Although his "empire" was really much of western Europe and did not even include all of Italy, he was the strongest ruler at the time, and therefore, in the minds of many people, the man who should be the new emperor.

European kings after Charlemagne based their laws on Roman laws. European universities made sure their students read Roman histories and Roman poets, such as Virgil. In later centuries, Rome was rediscovered as a center for art, culture, and learning. Although the empire ended, its power and influence continued to live on.

Charlemagne was crowned emperor in 800 CE by Pope Leo III.

Chapter 17
The Heritage of Greece and Rome

A Rich Legacy It is almost impossible to overestimate the influence the civilizations of Greece and Rome have had on American civilization. If you visit our nation's capital, you will see that the great majority of our important national buildings and monuments are based on Greek and Roman architecture.

The Lincoln Memorial was inspired by the Parthenon. The White House, the Jefferson Memorial, the Supreme Court, and the Capitol are all based on

Greek and Roman designs. In fact, it is rare to find a statehouse anywhere in the country that is not based, at least in part, on **classical** architecture. Many older banks and churches also show traces of the classical style.

But these buildings are only the tip of the iceberg. Our political institutions have also been greatly influenced by these ancient cultures. The leaders of the American Revolution and the framers of the U.S. Constitution paid close attention to the political histories of Greece and Rome. They didn't want the American states to be as disunited as the ancient Greek city-states. However, they also didn't want the national government to be as strong and centralized

The architectural style of the Supreme Court building in Washington, DC, was based on classical architecture.

as it was under the Roman Empire. In laying out the Constitution, they tried to create a mixed government. They tried to make sure that different parts of the government serve as "checks and balances" against one other. They paid particularly close attention to the Roman Republic.

As a result, we have a government that borrows heavily from the Romans. We pledge allegiance to a republic inspired by the Roman Republic. We elect senators to a Senate modeled partly on the Roman Senate. But we have borrowed from the Greeks as well. From them, we have taken the idea of democracy, the principle of majority rule, and the concept of a jury. Even our major political parties—Democratic and Republican—can trace their names back to ancient Greece and Rome.

The cultural influence of ancient Greece and Rome is with us not only on election day but every day of the year. Although many people may not realize it, our calendar is basically a Roman calendar, designed by Julius Caesar. Several of our months are named for Roman gods, and two summer months are named for Julius Caesar and Augustus Caesar.

The way we divide our day into a.m. and p.m. also comes from the Romans. The Romans divided the day into two parts: the time before the sun reaches its meridian, or middle point, and the time after the sun passes the meridian. In Latin (the language of ancient Rome), these periods are referred to as *ante meridiem*, or a.m., and *post meridiem*, or p.m.

Nor are these the only abbreviations that come from the Latin language. Do you know anyone who has a B.A. degree? Or maybe an M.A., M.D., J.D., or Ph.D.? All of these abbreviations come from Latin. And so do some others you might see in books. The abbreviation *e.g.* (*exempli gratia*) means "for example"; *i.e.* (*id est*) means "that is"; and *n.b.* (*nota bene*) means "note well."

Greek and Latin Words

Thousands of English words are derived from Latin words. English also includes many Greek words, many of which you have already encountered in this book. You probably speak several Latin and Greek words every day without even realizing it. Take a look at the chart. How many of these words do you know and use?

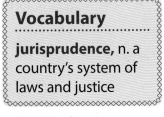

English Words from Latin	English Words from Greek
aquarium	aristocracy
army	astronomy
cancer	athlete
candle	comedy
cereal	democracy
extra	economics
gladiator	epic
hospital	geometry
jurisprudence	harmony
justice	hero
language	laconic
major	marathon
minor	mathematics
nebula	melody
picture	metaphor
pirate	olympics
pollen	panic
port	philosophy
prejudice	physics
property	poetry
radius	police officer
salary	politics
school	rhetoric
senate	rhythm
street	spartan
verb	stadium
vision	tragedy

Of course, all of this might have turned out differently. If the Athenians and the Spartans had not cooperated to force the Persians out of Greece during the Persian Wars, the Persians might have conquered much of Europe and our language might be full of Persian words. We might not think about politics, drama, or architecture in the same way that we do today. Likewise, if Carthage had burned Rome to the ground, both our language and our culture would certainly be different. But those things did not happen. Instead, it was the civilizations of Greece and Rome that prevailed and prospered. These two civilizations had a great influence on the European cultures that came after them, and European immigrants eventually brought their cultures to America.

The knowledge and accomplishments of the ancient Greeks and Romans laid the groundwork for many of the achievements of later centuries. Engineering achievements, such as the column and the arch, made it possible to build cathedrals, palaces, law courts, and government buildings, as well as bridges

The ancient Greeks loved theater. Inspired by the ancient Greeks, there are outdoor theaters in many parts of the world. This outdoor theater is in Cornwall, England.

and towers. History made it possible to understand and learn from the past, while philosophy and religion made it easier to understand the universe. Drama and art made life more enjoyable; government made it more orderly; medicine and science helped extend it.

All these things, taken together, make up the cultural **heritage** of ancient Greece and Rome. They represent a tradition, or a collection of ideas and concepts that we have inherited from these earlier cultures. The Greco-Roman heritage is so rich, and so important, that it is impossible to fully understand modern America without knowing a little about ancient Greece and Rome. That is why these ancient civilizations are still important today.

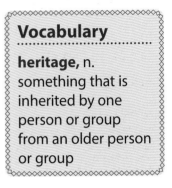

Vocabulary

heritage, n. something that is inherited by one person or group from an older person or group

Many of our ideas of government can be traced to ancient Greece. The democratic principle of people choosing their own leaders is demonstrated during local, state, and national elections when candidates are chosen.

Glossary

A

abstract, adj. relating to ideas, rather than concrete objects, actions, or people (68)

administrator, n. a person responsible for carrying out the day-to-day workings of an organization or government (110)

ally, n. a nation that promises to help another nation in wartime (38)

architect, n. a person who designs buildings (40)

aristocracy, n. the upper or noble class whose members' status is usually inherited (5)

"aristocratic council," (phrase) a group of people from the upper class or nobility who helped govern Sparta (21)

"aristocratic republic," (phrase) a government in which people from the upper class or nobility serve as representatives (84)

Asia Minor, n. a peninsula in southwestern Asia; today most of this area is the country of Turkey (2)

assassinate, v. to kill someone; often a ruler or member of the government (72)

assassination, n. the murder of a public figure, such as a government official (106)

assembly, n. a group of people; in ancient Greece, the Assembly made laws (7)

B

baptize, v. to perform a ceremony that brings a person into the Christian Church (124)

barracks, n. buildings where soldiers live (18)

C

citizen, n. a person who is legally recognized as a member or subject of a country or state (8)

city-state, n. a city that is an independent political state with its own ruling government (2)

civil war, n. a war between people who live in the same country (102)

classical, adj. belonging to, or in the style of, ancient Greece or Rome (136)

conspirator, n. a person who plans or participates with others in a crime (106)

conversion, n. a change in one's religious beliefs (124)

corruption, n. illegal or dishonest behavior, often by people in a position of power (11)

D

democracy, n. a in ancient Greece, a form of government in which the male citizens held ruling power and made decisions; in modern times, a form of government in which citizens choose the leaders by vote (5)

dialogue, n. a piece of writing organized as a conversation between two or more characters (64)

"diplomatic relations," (phrase) formal contact or communication between countries, including an exchange of representatives called diplomats (50)

dramatist, n. a person who writes plays (40)

E

economic, adj. relating to the management of money and resources to produce, buy, and sell goods and services (128)

edict, n. an official order given by a ruler (124)

emblem, n. a symbol (24)

"epic poem," (phrase) a long poem that tells the story of a hero's adventures (13)

ethics, n. rules based on ideas about right and wrong (58)

evacuate, v. to leave a place in an organized way, in order to get away from danger (34)

G

Gallic Wars, n. wars between Rome and the people of Gaul, which today is the country of France (101)

governor, n. the leader of the government in a province (87)

H

heir, n. a person who will legally receive the property of someone who dies; the person who will become king or queen after the current king or queen dies or steps down (79)

Hellenistic, adj. relating to Greek culture or language (79)

heritage, n. something that is inherited by one person or group from an older person or group (141)

hypocrite, n. a person whose behavior does not match his or her beliefs (59)

I

idealistic, adj. believing in high standards or the possibility of perfection (66)

immortalize, v. to honor a person or event by creating an artistic or literary work, causing the person or event to be remembered forever (26)

infantryman, n. a soldier who travels and fights on foot (74)

inflation, n. a rise in prices and a fall in the purchasing value of money (128)

J

jurisprudence, n. a country's system of laws and justice (139)

jury, n. a group of people who listen to information presented during a trial in a court and make decisions about whether someone is guilty or innocent (11)

L

landlocked, adj. cut off from the seacoast; surrounded by land (22)

league, n. a group that works together to achieve common goals (38)

legion, n. a group or unit of about three thousand to six thousand soldiers in the Roman army (114)

logic, n. the study of ways of thinking and making well-reasoned arguments (13)

M

mean, n. a place between two extremes; the middle (70)

miracle, n. an extraordinary event or action that is considered an act of God (120)

monarchy, n. a government led by a king or a queen (5)

O

oligarchy, n. a government controlled by a small group of people made up of aristocratic and wealthy non-aristocratic families (5)

orator, n. a skilled public speaker (39)

ostracize, v. in ancient Athens, to send a person away from the city; today, *ostracize* means to shun or ignore a person (10)

P

pagan, adj. related to the worship of many gods or goddesses (125)

pass, n. a place in the mountains that is lower than the surrounding peaks and that people use as a path through the mountains (33)

patrician, n. a member of ancient Rome's highest social class; a wealthy landowner in ancient Rome (85)

Pax Romana, n. literally, Roman peace; a period of about two hundred years without major conflicts in the Roman Empire (115)

persecution, n. cruel and unfair treatment of a group of people (123)

phalanx, n. a group of soldiers who attack in close formation with their shields overlapping and spears pointed forward (22)

phenomena, n. observable events; in nature, occurrences such as sun, rain, storms, and earthquakes **(56)**

philosophy, n. the study of ideas about knowledge, life, and truth; literally, love of wisdom **(54)**

Phoenicians, n. an ancient Mediterranean trading civilization **(90)**

plague, n. a highly contagious, usually fatal, disease that affects large numbers of people **(51)**

plebeian, n. a common person without power in ancient Rome **(85)**

plunder, v. to take something by force **(131)**

priestess, n. a woman who has the training or authority to carry out certain religious ceremonies or rituals **(27)**

prominence, n. importance; fame **(72)**

propaganda, n. false or exaggerated information that is spread to encourage belief in a certain person or idea **(113)**

prophet, n. someone chosen by God to bring a message to people **(132)**

province, n. an area or region; when an area was conquered by Rome, it became a province under Roman control **(87)**

Punic, adj. Carthaginian; the Roman word *punicus* is Latin for Phoenician, and the Carthaginians were descendants of the Phoenicians **(90)**

R

reason, n. the ability of the mind to think and understand **(56)**

recession, n. a time of reduced economic activity, when there is little buying or selling **(128)**

rhetoric, n. the skill of using words effectively in speaking or writing **(13)**

rite, n. a ritual or ceremony **(29)**

ritual, n. an act or series of actions done in the same way in a certain situation, such as a religious ceremony **(122)**

"rock quarry," (phrase) a place where stones are taken from the earth **(52)**

S

sophist, n. a philosopher; in ancient Greece, a teacher of philosophy and rhetoric **(60)**

soul, n. the nonphysical part of a person; in many religions, the soul is believed to live even after the body dies **(57)**

spoils, n. property or valuables taken by the winner in a conflict **(115)**

statesman, n. a political leader **(46)**

T

trade route, n. a road or waterway traveled by merchants or traders to buy or sell goods **(96)**

treasury, n. a place where the money and other riches of a government are kept **(115)**

tribune, n. in ancient Rome, an elected plebeian representative **(85)**

tribute, n. payment of money or goods by a people or their ruler to another country or ruler, in exchange for protection **(88)**

Trojans, n. people from the ancient city of Troy in Asia Minor **(112)**

truce, n. an agreement to stop fighting **(24)**

tyranny, n. a type of government in which one person illegally seizes all power, usually ruling in a harsh and brutal way; a dictatorship **(5)**

V

virtue, n. a high moral standard **(67)**

Core Knowledge®

CKHG™
Core Knowledge HISTORY AND GEOGRAPHY™

Series Editor-In-Chief
E.D. Hirsch, Jr.

Editorial Directors
Linda Bevilacqua and Rosie McCormick

Subject Matter Expert

Michael J. Carter, PhD, Professor,
Department of Classics, Brock University

Illustration and Photo Credits

A Roman Legion (gouache on paper), Linklater, Barrie (b.1931) / Private Collection / © Look and Learn / Bridgeman Images: 114

A Spartan hoplite, or heavy armed soldier (gouache on paper), Howat, Andrew (20th Century) / Private Collection / Bridgeman Images: Cover A, 17

A young woman arranging her clothes in a coffer, 450 BC (stone), Greek, (5th century BC) / Museo Archeologico Nazionale, Taranto, Puglia, Italy / Bridgeman Images: 12

Aristotle and Plato: detail of School of Athens, 1510–11 (fresco) (detail of 472), Raphael (Raffaello Sanzio of Urbino) (1483–1520) / Vatican Museums and Galleries, Vatican City / Bridgeman Images: 69

Assault on Carthage (gouache on paper), Baraldi, Severino (b.1930) / Private Collection / © Look and Learn / Bridgeman Images: 95

Athenian trireme, Howat, Andrew (20th Century) / Private Collection / © Look and Learn / Bridgeman Images: 31

Aureus of Constantine the Great (AD 306–37) Emperor of Rome, Trier Mint, AD 306–37 (obverse) (gold), Roman, (4th century AD) / Fitzwilliam Museum, University of Cambridge, UK / Bridgeman Images: 128

Battle of Marathon, Payne, Roger (b.1934) / Private Collection / © Look and Learn / Bridgeman Images: 36–37

Battle of Salamis, Howat, Andrew (20th Century) / Private Collection / © Look and Learn / Bridgeman Images: 35

Brian Jannsen/age fotostock/SuperStock: 42

Bust of Alcibiades (c.450–04 BC) (marble), Greek School / Musei Capitolini, Rome, Italy / Bridgeman Images: 53

Bust of greek general and politician Pericles, Roman copy in marble of Greek original from the Acropolis in Athens (Greece), Greek Civilization, 5th Century BC / De Agostini Picture Library / G. Nimatallah / Bridgeman Images: 39

Bust of Plato (c.428–c.348 BC) (stone), Greek / Musei Capitolini, Rome, Italy / Bridgeman Images: 67

Bust of Sophocles (496–406 BC) (marble), Roman / Musei Capitolini, Rome, Italy / Bridgeman Images: 46

Cimon takes command of the Greek Fleet, illustration from 'Hutchinson's History of the Nations', 1915 (litho), Weatherstone, A.C. (fl.1888–1929) / Private Collection / The Stapleton Collection / Bridgeman Images: 23

Constantinople / Biblioteca Nacional, Madrid, Spain / Photo © AISA / Bridgeman Images: 133

Debate in the early Roman senate (gouache on paper), Baraldi, Severino (b.1930) / Private Collection / © Look and Learn / Bridgeman Images: 105

Detail from the eastern frieze of the Parthenon showing part of the Assemlby of the Gods / Werner Forman Archive / Bridgeman Images: 4

Emperor Augustus (63 BC–14 AD) (stone), Roman / Galleria degli Uffizi, Florence, Italy / Bridgeman Images: Cover E, 109

Emperor Constantine I (c.274–337) the Great (mosaic), Byzantine / San Marco, Venice, Italy / Bridgeman Images: 125

f.106r The Coronation of Emperor Charlemagne (742–814) by Pope Leo III (c.750–816) at St. Peters, Rome in 800, Grandes Chroniques de France, 1375–79 (vellum), French School, (14th century) / Bibliotheque Municipale, Castres, France / Bridgeman Images: 135

Figurine of a girl running, (bronze), Greek, (6th century BC) / British Museum, London, UK / Bridgeman Images: 18

George Munday/age fotostock/SuperStock: 8–9

Gold Stater, Alexander the Great coinage of Sicyon, c.323 BC (obverse) / Fitzwilliam Museum, University of Cambridge, UK / Bridgeman Images: Cover B, 76

Great Fire of Rome in 64 AD (gouache on paper), Baraldi, Severino (b.1930) / Private Collection / © Look and Learn / Bridgeman Images: 130

Greece, Athens, The Acropolis of Athens, Dionysus Theatre,4th Century BC, Ancient Greece / De Agostini Picture Library / G. Dagli Orti / Bridgeman Images: 44

Greece, Corinth, Apollo Temple,6th Century BC, Ancient Greece / De Agostini Picture Library / G. Dagli Orti / Bridgeman Images: 48–49

Hannibal crossing the Alps, English School, (20th century) / Private Collection / © Look and Learn / Bridgeman Images: 93

Heraclitus of Ephesus (c.535–c.475 BC) (oil on canvas), French School, (17th century) (after) / Bibliotheque de la Faculte de Medecine, Paris, France / Archives Charmet / Bridgeman Images: 57

Ian Cook/Image Source/SuperStock: 29

Iberfoto/SuperStock: 89

imageBROKER/SuperStock: 140

In earliest times a simple foot-race was the only event, illustration from The Story of Greece by Mary Macgregor, 1st edition, 1913 (colour print), Crane, Walter (1845–1915) / Private Collection / The Stapleton Collection / Bridgeman Images: 25

Ingemar Edfalk/Blend Images/SuperStock: 141

Julius Caesar crosses the Rubicon (colour litho), English School, (20th century) / Private Collection / © Look and Learn / Bridgeman Images: Cover D, 103

Leonidas and his troops fighting to the end, English School, (20th century) / Private Collection / © Look and Learn / Bridgeman Images: 33

Masters and pupils at the Athenian school where studies included music. Greek red figure vessel. Staatliche Museum Berlin / Universal History Archive/UIG / Bridgeman Images: 14

Olympic victor being crowned, illustration from 'Newnes' Pictorial Knowledge', 1932 (litho), English School, (20th century) / Private Collection / © Look and Learn / Bridgeman Images: 26

Ostrakon with the name of Themistokles, c.472 BC (ceramic), Greek, (5th century BC) / Agora Museum, Athens, Greece / Bridgeman Images: 10

Panathenaic black figure amphora depicting a foot race (pottery), Greek, (5th century BC) / Musee Municipal Antoine Vivenel, Compiegne, France / Bridgeman Images: Cover C, 25

Pericles delivering the funeral oration over the Athenians (litho), English School, (19th century) / Private Collection / The Stapleton Collection / Bridgeman Images: 51

Pheidippides bringing news to Athens in 490 BC, Salinas, Alberto (1932–2004) / Private Collection / © Look and Learn / Bridgeman Images: 32

Relief of a Trireme (stone), Greek School / Acropolis Museum, Athens, Greece / Bridgeman Images: 31 Robertharding/SuperStock

Roman civilization, Mosaic known as 'Alexander Mosaic' and depicting battle of Issus between armies of Alexander Great and Darius III of Persia, Copy of painting by Philoxenos of Eretria, From House of Faun, Pompei, Italy, / De Agostini Picture Library / G. Nimatallah / Bridgeman Images: 75

Roman Forum (colour litho), Italian School / Private Collection / De Agostini Picture Library / Bridgeman Images: 118–119

Roman Republican Coin from Rome, 44 BC (silver), Roman, (1st century BC) / Ashmolean Museum, University of Oxford, UK / Bridgeman Images: 104

Roman road construction (gouache on paper), Jackson, Peter (1922–2003) / Private Collection / © Look and Learn / Bridgeman Images: 127

Rome invaded by the Barbarians, Scarpelli, Tancredi (1866–1937) / Private Collection / © Look and Learn / Bridgeman Images: 132

Scholars at work in the famed library of Alexandria, Hook, Richard (b.1938) / Private Collection / © Look and Learn / Bridgeman Images: 80

Socrates Addressing the Athenians, illustration from 'Hutchinson's History of the Nations', 1915 (litho), Heath, Dudley (20th Century) / Private Collection / Bridgeman Images: 59

Socrates, marble head, copy from a bronze from the Pompeion in Athens, made by Lysippus, Classical Greek, c.330 BC / Louvre, Paris, France / Bridgeman Images: 58

Spartan Army, Howat, Andrew (20th Century) / Private Collection / © Look and Learn / Bridgeman Images: 20

Spartan warrior (bronze), Greek, (6th century BC) / Private Collection / Photo © Boltin Picture Library / Bridgeman Images: 17

St. Paul Preaching at Athens (cartoon for the Sistine Chapel) (PRE RESTORATION), Raphael (Raffaello Sanzio of Urbino) (1483–1520) / Victoria & Albert Museum, London, UK / Bridgeman Images: 121

The academy at Athens (colour litho), English School, (20th century) / Private Collection / © Look and Learn / Bridgeman Images: 65

The Acropolis and Parthenon, Payne, Roger (b.1934) / Private Collection / © Look and Learn / Bridgeman Images: 54–55

The Alexander Mosaic, detail depicting the Darius III (399-330 BC) at the Battle of Issus against Alexander the Great (356-323 BC) in 333 BC (mosaic) (detail of 154003), Roman, (1st century BC) / Museo Archeologico Nazionale, Naples, Italy / Bridgeman Images: 72–73

The Arch of Titus, Rome (w/c on paper), Wyld, William (1806–89) / Manchester Art Gallery, UK / Bridgeman Images: 84

The Battle of Alexander at Issus. Oil painting by the German artist Albrecht Altdorfer (1480–1538). 1529. Detail., Altdorfer, Albrecht (c.1480–1538) / Alte Pinakothek, Munich, Germany / Photo © Tarker / Bridgeman Images: 75

The death of Julius Caesar, Doughty, C.L. (1913–85) / Private Collection / © Look and Learn / Bridgeman Images: 107

The Death of Socrates, 1787 (oil on canvas), David, Jacques Louis (1748–1825) / Metropolitan Museum of Art, New York, USA / Bridgeman Images: 62

The Discobolus of Myron. Greek sculpture. From The National Encyclopaedia, published c.1890. / Private Collection / Photo © Ken Welsh / Bridgeman Images: 28

The early city of Rome, Baraldi, Severino (b.1930) / Private Collection / © Look and Learn / Bridgeman Images: 82–83

The Parthenon, built 447-432 BC (photo) / Acropolis, Athens, Greece / © SGM / Bridgeman Images: i, iii, 41

The Parthenon, the Proylaea and the Erechtheum, Athens, built in the 5th century BC (photo) / Acropolis, Athens, Greece / Photo © AISA / Bridgeman Images: 55

The School of Athens, from the Stanza della Segnatura, 1509–10 (fresco), Raphael (Raffaello Sanzio of Urbino) (1483–1520) / Vatican Museums and Galleries, Vatican City / Bridgeman Images: 69

The Toreador Fresco, Knossos Palace, Crete, c.1500 BC (fresco) / National Archaeological Museum, Athens, Greece / Bridgeman Images: 2–3

The Wrestler, copy of Greek sculpture 3rd century BC (marble) (see also 122614) / Galleria degli Uffizi, Florence, Italy / Bridgeman Images: 28

Triumph of Faith – Christian Martyrs in the Time of Nero, 65 AD (oil on canvas), Thirion, Eugene Romain (1839–1910) / Private Collection / Photo © Bonhams, London, UK / Bridgeman Images: 123

Urn depicting a wedding scene, red-figure pottery from Illyria, Albania. Greek civilization, 4th Century BC. / De Agostini Picture Library / A. De Gregorio / Bridgeman Images: 47

Vercingetorix throws down his arms at the feet of Julius Caesar, 1899 (oil on canvas), Royer, Lionel Noel (1852–1926) / Musee Crozatier, Le Puy-en-Velay, France / Bridgeman Images: 101

View of the exterior showing the stairway, 13th-9th century BC (photo), Roman / Ara Pacis (Altar of Peace), Rome, Italy / Bridgeman Images: 110

Virgil (70-19 BC) and the Muses, from Sousse (Hadrumetum) (mosaic), Roman, (3rd century AD) / Musee National du Bardo, Le Bardo, Tunisia / Bridgeman Images: 1, 112

Walter Bibikow/age fotostock/SuperStock: 137

When They Were Young: The Great General Hannibal, Jackson, Peter (1922–2003) / Private Collection / © Look and Learn / Bridgeman Images: 92